HOLLAND COMPASS

the Netherlands Unesco centre

We gladly recommend "Holland Compass" as a valuable socio-historical publication.

Holland Compass especially aroused our interest because of the way all the Dutch listed monuments on the UNESCO World Heritage List are highlighted like pearls in their relevant context taking water as the common theme.

Holland Compass comes in a handy format: it is easy to take on one's travels and yet it is a rich source of reference material. Considering the quality of information and presentation, we are convinced that this publication will be enjoyed by a broad public.

(Mrs) Mathilde C. Guurink,

director Unesco Centre in the Netherlands.

HOLLAND COMPASS

F.S. Hoep

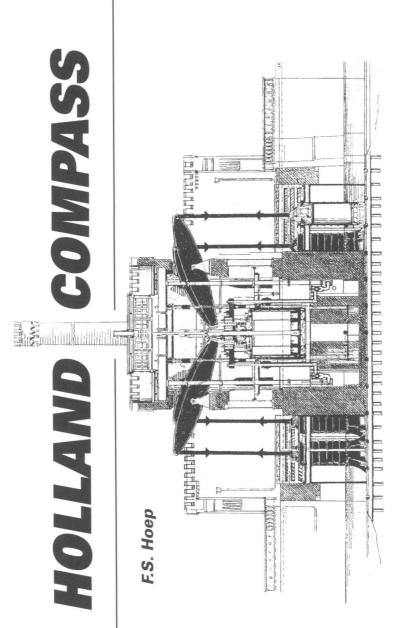

Holland Compass is a publication of Communicatie Bureau Hoep & Partners, Haarlem.
© Copyright 2002. ISBN 90-801454-2-4

Contents

Introduction

Creating land from water

The name "Holland" may well have originated in the Haarlem region. This area of predominantly willow woodland was referred to as "Houtland". Records show that the name "Holtland" which formed the basis for the later term Holland was in use certainly prior to the year 1200. Currently the Netherlands has an area of thirty-four thousand square kilometres.

The western provinces are below sea level. Were these not protected by sea defences then half the country would be underwater. It is significant that about three-quarters of the Dutch population lives in these provinces. In the absence of dikes, the city of Amersfoort for instance would be by the sea, and the coastline would shift eastwards as far as the Drentse Heuvelrug (Drente Ridge).

Map of the Netherlands in the absence of dikes or seadefences and a water level of zero N(ew) A(msterdam) P(watermark)

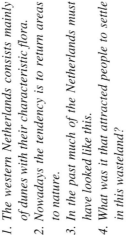

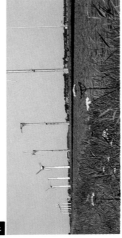

1. The western Netherlands consists mainly of dunes with their characteristic flora.
2. Nowadays the tendency is to return areas to nature.
3. In the past much of the Netherlands must have looked like this.
4. What was it that attracted people to settle in this wasteland?
5. Modern windmills.

It would continue along the northern boundary of the Veluwe and further via the Utrechtse Heuvelrug (Utrecht Ridge) in the direction of the Drunense Duinen (Drunen Dunes). In the following chapters we will see how the ingenuity of the Lowlanders in regulating water has continued to flourish to the present day giving them a leading position in the field of water management.

1 The history of the country's formation

The Netherlands is situated by the sea at the mouth of the rivers Rhine and Meuse. Its origin is that of a desolate region subject to frequent flooding. The inhabitants of the lowlying areas often took refuge on raised mounds.

The Netherlands in 7000 BC

Prehistory

The geological history of the earth is based on a time-scale of some 600 million years. The formation of the Lowlands began only two million years ago. This period is known by geologists as the "Quaternary".

The Ice Age

The Quaternary Period is divided into Pleistocene and Holocene. The Pleistocene is a period of cold characterised by the Ice Ages. There were three of these consisting of cold periods of varying intensity. The ground was frozen throughout the year and in the summer the temperature rarely rose above 0°C. The penultimate Ice Age (180.000 to 130.000 years ago) was the most severe.

An enormous ice cap formed in the North and reached as far south as the central

The study of skeletal remains tells us what the extinct mammoth must have looked like.

The oldest dunes formed on beach-ridges and wind erosion created younger dunes.

The hunebedden (barrows) made by man in the Early Stone Age (1200-1400 BC).

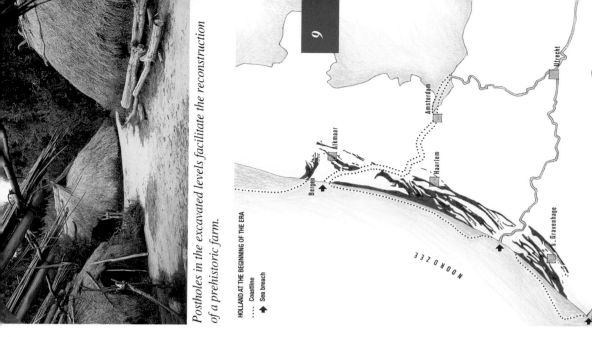

Postholes in the excavated levels facilitate the reconstruction of a prehistoric farm.

HOLLAND AT THE BEGINNING OF THE ERA
···· Coastline
↑ Sea breach

N O O R D Z E E

Bergen
Alkmaar
Amsterdam
Haarlem
Utrecht
S. Gravenhage
Rotterdam

Netherlands (the line running from Haarlem through Utrecht to Nijmegen). Sea level at that time was tens of metres lower than the present day level. England was connected by land to the Continent.

The frontal and lateral pressures exerted by the ice mass were such that moraines were activit created. The formation of areas such as the Gooi, Utrechtse Heuvelrug, Veluwe and the Hondsrug in Drenthe are all due to this glacial activity.

In the last Ice Age the ice sheet no longer reached as far south as the Netherlands. But it was so cold that the only vegetation was a layer of tundra-like plants covering the ground. Then about 10.000 years ago the temperature started to rise heralding the dawn of the Holocene period. The sea rose to such a level as to isolate the British Isles. There was however no question of a regular rise in sea level. Sometimes the sea receded (regression) only to return to claim back even more land than before (transgression). In the Holocene period the first hunters and fishers established themselves in Holland and this period is still continuing today.

The beach-ridges

The fact that our coastline was on a gentle slope with a southwest current running parallel to it, meant that an onshore wind would create long stretches of sand ridges (strandwal). Between these series of ridges rich marshland vegetation grew up.

About 5000 years ago the coastline was established on its current alignment but about 10 kilometres further east. Between 4300 and 3500 BC a series of new beach ridges was laid down as the sea retreated in a westerly direction.

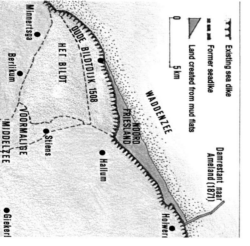

Demographic development of the northern coastal provinces

Human settlement of artificial mounds took place in the northern provinces in the period 500 BC to 1000 AD. The form of the landscape was largely determined by the sea. In the course of history the sea has not only taken away land but has also created it. In the northern part of Groningen and Friesland, bordering the Waddenzee, silting of the mudflats gradually created new land. At high tide clay was naturally deposited and as a result this raised land was no longer inundated. Vegetation consolidated

The mound culture
In the period from the 7th century BC to ca.1000/AD the inhabitants of the northern region of the Netherlands developed their settlements on artificial mounds.
The map shows the highest concentration of mounds occurring in modern Friesland

LAND RECLAMATION AROUND MIDDELZEE.

Legend:
- ┬┬┬ Existing sea dike
- ┄┄┄ Former seadike
- ▲ Land created from mud flats

0 ――― 5 km

Damrestant naar" Ameland (1871)

Places on map: Minnertsga, Berlikum, OUDE BILDTDIJK 1508, HET BILDT, NOORD FRIESLAND, WADDENZEE, 'VOORMALIGE 'MIDDELZEE, Stiens, Hallum, Holwert, Giekerl

the new land and it was then a simple matter for the inhabitants to erect a dike as extra protection against flooding. The land thus reclaimed was integrated into the adjoining farm and this came to be known as the law of "opstrek". This process led to a pattern of irregular plots with occasional cross dikes which can still be seen in today's landscape. The more recent clay polders resulting from reclamation activity by the inhabitants are also to be found in this coastal region. These plots are divided in a more regular pattern. This area of Friesland originally stretched much further along the coast in a northeasterly direction as far as Bremen. Study of the topographical situation shown on an old

Mound at Hogebeintum, highest in the land.

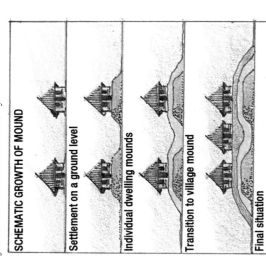

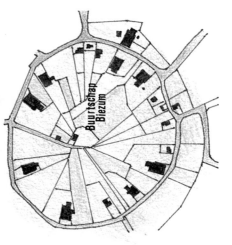

At ebb tide the Wadden is laid dry.

Waddenzee lies to the south of the chain of islands. At the start of the era the islands were part of the mainland. In the course of time the sea encroached more and more into the area behind the coast forming what we now know as the wadden. At low tide the wadden are practically laid dry. At high tide the sea forces its way through the narrow inlets between the islands and the wadden are flooded. Further south along the Friesian coast of the former Zuider Zee is the beautiful rolling landscape of Gaasterland. This area was formed during the Ice Age when the alluvium bed was raised by the overriding ice masses. Cliffs were formed along this coast when the battering waves caused sections of alluvium to break away.

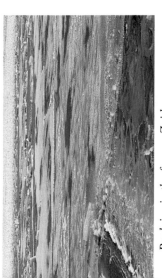

Pack ice in the former Zuiderzee.

"mound map" of the Netherlands reveals that the sea clay region of Friesland was divided into two parts by a sea inlet known as the Middelzee.

Around 1000 AD monks in the area were already involved in land reclamation. In 1508 colonists from Holland reclaimed the mouth of the inlet. In the subsequent period 1605 -1754 an additional 5500 hectares of mud flats were reclaimed by the construction of an enclosing dike. On the map of Friesland this area is called " Het Bildt" Off the coast of Friesland lie the Wadden islands of Texel,Terschelling, Vlieland, Ameland, Schiermonnikoog and Rottum. The North Sea coast of the islands is lined with sand dunes, which are covered in woodland on their inland flank. The

The enclosure pattern of a mound can be compared to the spokes of a cartwheel.

Unfortunately a number of these archaeological landscape features were lost for their fertile soil in the 19th century.

SCHEMATIC GROWTH OF MOUND

Settlement on a ground level

Individual dwelling mounds

Transition to village mound

Final situation

The sea dunes are a vulnerable feature.

Also these plants are capable of consolidating the sand with their root systems and they spread to cover the flanks of the dunes.

The young dunes

Around 1200 the western coastline was inundated by the sea. It is possible that the inhabitants themselves were partly to blame since they had cleared the natural vegetation for their own use. The result was a high degree of erosion and the advance of the coastline in an easterly direction. The most significant shifting of sand took place in the period between the 13th and the 17th centuries. The old dune formations were covered with a new layer of sand thus creating the landscape of the young dunes that we know today.

Demographic development

It goes without saying that the original inhabitants of the coastal region would settle on the higher land. A number of towns and villages in the coastal provinces can trace their origin and location to these extensive ridges of sand. At first the activities of the sea in this region were unimpeded. Even the course of the rivers here was subject to change. In Roman times the mouth of the Rhine was at Katwijk. The whole of the area to the north of Amsterdam consisted of one large lake

Demographic development of the western coast provinces

The coasts of Holland and Zeeland consist of sand dune and beach. At a number of locations the government has had to consolidate the dunes and strengthen them with dikes as a protection against the everthreatening sea. The sea dunes are our oldest natural sea defence.

The old dunes

About 4,300 years ago the onshore wind gradually built up a 10 metres high series of low dunes perched on top of the previously mentioned beach ridges. Small obstructions were sufficient to give the sand a foothold. Dune forming plants such as rye grass and bent grass are excellent survivors in a salt environment (marram).

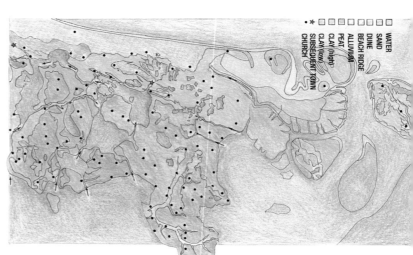

WATER
SAND
DUNE
BEACH RIDGE
ALLUVIUM
PEAT
CLAY (high)
CLAY (low)
SUBSEQUENT TOWN
CHURCH

Drawing based on map of Beekman

Nature reserve at the tip of North-Holland.

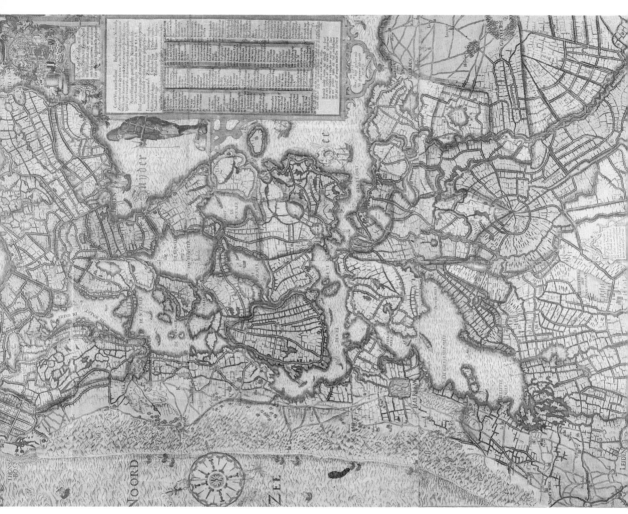

Historical map by Joost Janszoon, engraver 1575 (right) and a copy omitting reclaimed land (left) show how vulnerable and easily penetrable by the sea the northern extremity of Holland would have been had the West Friesian ringdike not been functioning as a sea defence. This dike protected the inhabitants from just such a disaster.

directly connected to the sea. The settlement of Schagen to the north of Alkmaar lay practically by the sea. It is clear that had there not been a wave of dike-building activity around the year 1000, the sea behind the dunes would have become one extensive area of wadden. Between the year 1000 and the beginning of the 16th century, a vast programme of reclamation gained momentum. Contemporary colonists were awarded licences to farm the peat bogs. These settlers began by digging drainage ditches which resulted in settlement of the ground. To make matters worse they began to cut the peat to supply the demands of the growing towns for heating fuel. Extensive areas of the country settled to below sea level. In fact the inhabitants were unwittingly contributing to their own vulnerability. Dike construction and forced drainage became a bitter necessity.

The South-Holland and Zeeland islands

These islands at the mouth of the river delta are a result of dike construction and the ensuing silting. Old maps of this island region show how almost every half-century the islands change shape or even disappear completely. Like the other lowlying parts of the coastal provinces at the beginning of the era, this was also a region of extensive peat bogs. On the seaward flank dune formation took place on the beach ridge. The rivers flowed via narrow channels into the sea. In 350 AD the sea dunes were breached by a storm tide. At several locations the peat was washed away. Creeks were formed among islands of peat and the sea and rivers left behind a deposit of clay. Around 800 the influence of the sea waned and the floods receded. The creeks began to silt up. These creek beds can still be recognised in the landscape today, and they were the first features used for settlements. The collapsed peat beds are called "poelgronden or wetlands" and these were used for cattle raising.

Map of Zeeland around 1300. The inset shows an area of mudflats in Zeeland called "schorren".

Mudflats in Zeeland

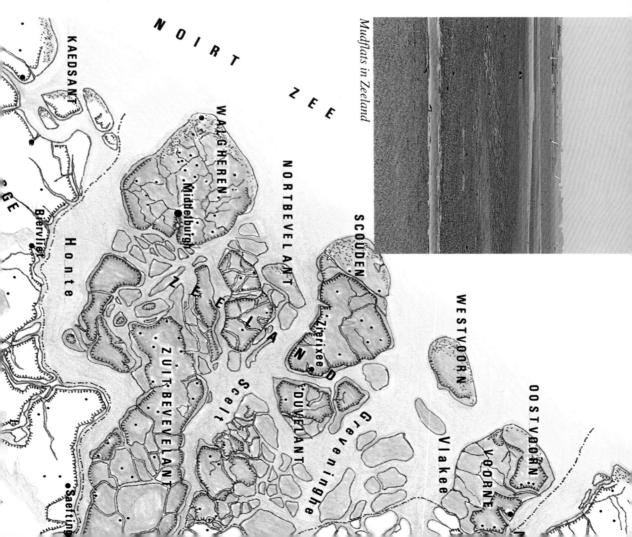

A panoramic view of the river IJssel at Doesburg. The IJssel, a tributary of the Rhine, flows into the IJsselmeer.

The river delta region

For a thousand years the rivers Rhine Meuse and Waal have determined the landscape of this region. These rivers have their source in the highlands of Europe and transport their meltwater and precipitation to our region. The river Rhine eventually broke through its banks between Arnhem and Nijmegen and found a shorter route to the sea. In the summer the rivers flowed in a narrow bedding.

As the supply of water increased the river became wider and occupied the "winter bed". The first inhabitants settled on the high embankments along the riverbanks. They used the fertile ground of the flood plains, deposited every year in the form of river clay, for rearing their cattle. Around the beginning of the second century the inhabitants started to build river dikes to influence the course of the river somewhat and to protect their farms.

Around 1300 the rivers in Gelderland were practically all provided with dikes. During the course of history the rivers have repeatedly broken their banks. The inhabitants have experienced many anxious moments in severe winters when the packice of the frozen river can force its way through the dike. They had no other option but to flee for their lives when this happened, and more often than not were overtaken by the pursuing floodwater.

Gradually the low-lying marshlands behind the dikes were cultivated. Ditches and canals were dug to drain away the water. As a result of this drainage and aeration of the ground, as in other parts of the country, settlement of the land took place. The subsidence was most dangerous directly behind the dikes, posing a threat to the inhabitants. The latest floods in the Betuwe were in 1926 and as a result an extensive programme of dike strengthening has been put in hand to prevent further breaching.

A separate chapter devoted to flood disasters demonstrates the need for continual vigilance in this respect.

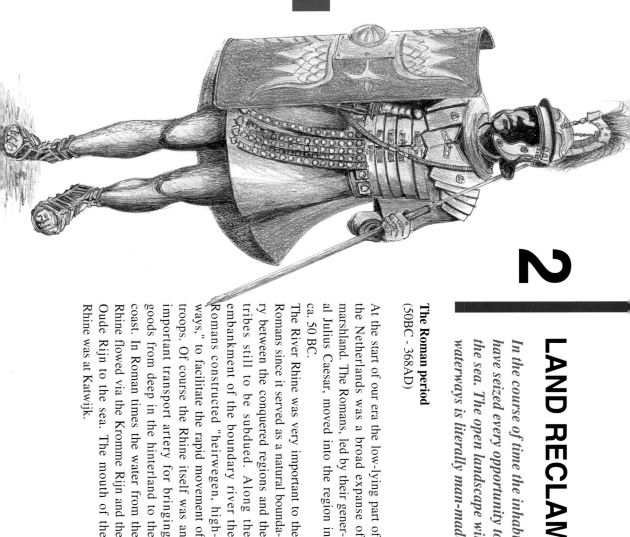

2 | LAND RECLAMATION

In the course of time the inhabitants of the Lowlands have seized every opportunity to claim back land from the sea. The open landscape with its dikes and waterways is literally man-made.

The Roman period
(50BC - 368AD)

At the start of our era the low-lying part of the Netherlands was a broad expanse of marshland. The Romans, led by their general Julius Caesar, moved into the region in ca. 50 BC.

The River Rhine was very important to the Romans since it served as a natural boundary between the conquered regions and the tribes still to be subdued. Along the embankment of the boundary river the Romans constructed "heirwegen, highways," to facilitate the rapid movement of troops. Of course the Rhine itself was an important transport artery for bringing goods from deep in the hinterland to the coast. In Roman times the water from the Rhine flowed via the Kromme Rijn and the Oude Rijn to the sea. The mouth of the Rhine was at Katwijk.

The fort Brittenburg was built by the Romans on the coast. It was later engulfed by the sea.

To the north of the Rhine boundary lived German tribes, the Batavians, Chamavi and Friesians. Two different worlds, that of the Romans and that of the Germans, existed in the region side-by-side. Even today the Dutch refer to the regions of the country as being either "above" or "below" the river delta.

Roman settlement

Roads were constructed to connect the raised settlements. They usually ran parallel to the river. They were no more than raised foundations using gravel from the riverbed and cannot be described as dikes. The river embankments offered the best protection from flooding and this is why the Romans built their settlements here.

Roman hydraulic engineering

The Romans first engineering activity was concerned with shipping movements. They constructed the Drusus Dam at the divergence of Rhine and Waal to divert more water into the Rhine. This improved both the strategic and navigational value of the river. They dug the Drusus Canal, which was probably located in the vicinity of Utrecht, to connect the Oude Rijn with the river Vecht. They also dug the Corbulo Canal across what is today the Province of South-Holland to link the river mouths of Oude Rijn and Meuse, a route followed by the present Rhine-Schie Canal. The original medieval bridge across the Meuse at Maastricht was a direct reference to its Roman predecessor. New forts were later added along the Rhine to serve as a base for conquering expeditions to places as far as the valley of the river Elbe.

Roman rule lasted till about 368 AD when the vast imperium began to crumble. This process led to the creation of the Eastern and Western Roman Empires.

Typical Roman buildings as reproduced in the Archeon at Alphen a/d Rijn.

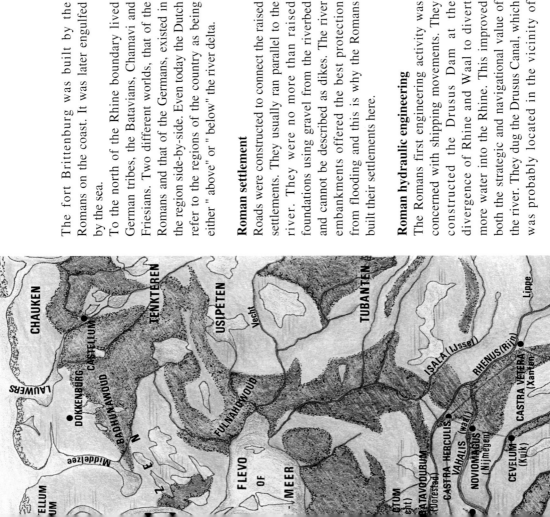

The Western Roman Empire with the river Rhine at its northern boundary was subject to constant attacks from the irrepressible German tribes. In an attempt to resist these attacks the emperor Valentinianus I strengthened the defences along the Meuse. This is the origin of the city of Nijmegen, or Noviomagnum as it was then called. That we know so much about this period of history is due to the work of the Roman historians. Modern excavations and the efforts of archaeologists are constantly bringing new facts to light. For instance in 1993 construction work on the Wijker tunnel near Velsen uncovered the remains of a Roman fort and harbour from 28 AD.

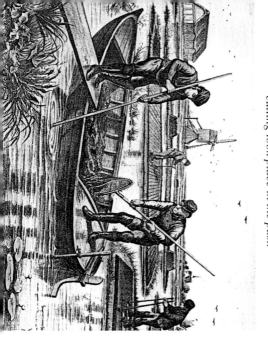

An old school picture illustrates how peat cutting took place in the past.

Nijmegen with its Valkhof demolished in 1795 is a good example of an early medieval city and bears witness to the time that Charles the Great stayed here.

The Middle-Ages (400 - 1400 AD)

The final demise of the Roman Empire ushered in the Middle Ages. In the coastal provinces the inhabitants had colonised the higher ground and lived from tilling crops, cattle rearing and fishing.

The working of the peat deposits lying between coast and inland sand ridges took place in the Carolingian Period (750 - 900). As mentioned previously this was an important activity providing fuel for heating.

Peat cutting

The systematic cutting of the peat first involved the digging of ditches to create strips of land 110 centimetres wide and 1250 metres long. Initially the dry peat was cut until the water table was reached. When a peat shortage arose, the wet peat was dug out using a dredging pole and laid out to dry (see illustration). As a result of this activity during the period 800 to 1250 deep lakes were created which grew in extent leading to extensive loss of land.

This drawing of the fortified tower at Middel-burg near Alkmaar is based on the excavated remains of foundations.

The fortified tower Radboud at Medemblik.

The West Friesian ring dike

Around the year one thousand the construction of a dike in West Friesland became urgent. The inhabitants of the North of Holland saw with trepidation how the water level in the North Sea and the Zuider zee were rising to frightening levels. It took two centuries to complete the ring dike which finally created a continuous sea defence. With its total length of 126 kilometres it was for the time it was built an impressive achievement. For Floris V, the Count of Holland at that time, it served a dual purpose.

It is assumed that the West Friesian ring dike was completed in around 1250. It formed a shield against the advancing sea.

Not only did it protect West Friesland from inundation, but by means of the six fortified towns he had built along its length, it also enabled the Count to control the rebellious West Friesians.

The ancient dike is still intact and connects the ports of Medemblik, Andijk, Enkhuizen and Hoorn all situated on the IJssel Lake. Inland it connects the towns of Alkmaar and Schagen with the coast. The dike is a structure of historical significance and bears witness to man's organisational ability and determination at that time.

KEY:

POSSIBLE LAND RECLAMATION
- 20th CENTURY
- 19th CENTURY
- 18th CENTURY
- 17th CENTURY
- 14th/16th CENTURY

Land reclamation

Due to the rapid increase in population and the growth of towns in the period 1500–1650 the demand for farming land was on the increase. A new era for land reclamation began with the introduction of windmills for the pumping of water. Initially the aristocracy took the initiative in the 16th century when van Egmond and Brederode concerned themselves with the draining of the Egmonder and Berger lakes near Alkmaar. In the 16 and 17th centuries, when the rich Amsterdam merchants realised the investment possibilities of land reclamation with the use of windmill power, the draining of deeper lakes to the north of Amsterdam became a priority. The Purmer and the Wormer lakes were tackled ten years later to be quickly followed by the Wijde Wormer and the Schermer. Around 1630 work was in progress on more than thirty drainage schemes.

The technique of reclamation was in essence very simple. A ring canal was dug around the lake, the ground from the excavation being used to raise a dike between canal and lake. The water was pumped from the lake into the canal using windmills and later steam pumps.

Egmond Lake near Alkmaar was drained in 1556, 590 hectares of land were reclaimed.

DRAINING THE SCHERMER IN FOUR STAGES

- sloten
- Snock mills (14)
- Lower mills (10)
- Middle mills (2)
- Lower & middle mills (2)
- Upper mills (14)

The Haarlem Lake

By the 19th century many lakes had been reclaimed, and it seemed as though the major tasks had been completed. Yet there was one location at the centre of the country where disaster still threatened. This was the Haarlemmermeer. In earlier times this lake had been essential for transport by water: it connected such towns as Amsterdam, Haarlem and Leiden. Small trading boats passing between north and south still made use of the lake to avoid having to use the sea coast route. The lake was also a source of fishing. But this large body of water continued to pose a threat for the

AREAS THREATENED WITH FLOODING SHOULD THE LEK DIKE COLLAPSE:

- 3 ground level above N.A.P.

areas threatened by flooding

reclaimed land

In the 16th & 17th centuries, North-Holland was the centre of land reclamation activity. During this period 27,000 hectares of land were reclaimed in North-Holland compared with 970 hectares in South-Holland. The division of Holland into northern and southern parts dates only from 1840. This topographical map of South-Holland shows just how extensive the area threatened with flooding would be should the dike along the Lek collapse.

Jan Adriaanszoon Leeghwater, builder of windmills.

surrounding region, especially when the prevailing southwesterly wind was driving the waves up high in the northeast corner. The airport's name "Schiphol" (ships hollow) bears witness to the dangers of this situation. To make matters worse, peat had been worked in the areas adjoining the lake, extending the water surface even further.

Draining the Haarlem Lake

In the 17th century the idea of draining the lake with the use of 166 windmills had been put forward by Leeghwater.

Old wooden lock from the 16th century built to maintain difference in water levels.

It is questionable whether the technology at the time was sufficiently advanced to achieve the tremendous task of utilising the necessary wind power. However the combined interests of shipping, fishing and water management prevented the draining of the lake. As a result the encroachment on the north eastern shore was such that the vast lake increasingly posed a threat for Amsterdam and the lowlying land as far as the river Amstel.

The steam age

In 1836 when the waters of the lake had advanced to the boundaries of Amsterdam and Leiden as a result of a storm, King Willem I decided to commission the reclaiming of the Haarlemmermeer.

In 1840 the government took a further decision to incorporate the use of steam power in the drainage plan. Work began on the excavation of a ring canal and the building of a ring dike. In 1849 pumping was commenced using three steam engines: the Leeghwater, the Lijnden and the Cruquius. In 1852 the tremendous task had been completed. During that period the pumps had transferred a total of 831.000.000 m3 of water into the ring canal.

The introduction of steam power was a boon for modern water management

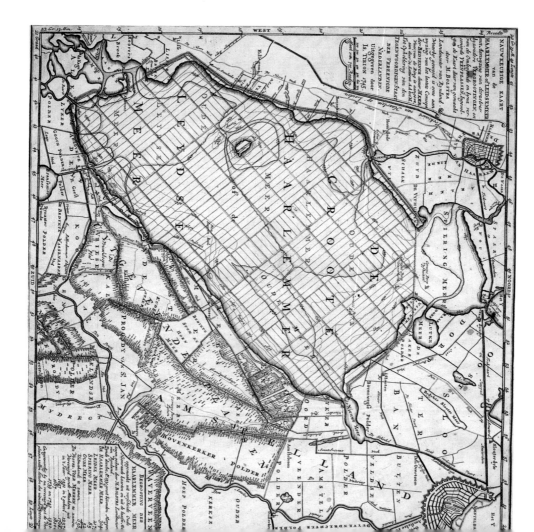

because it freed the pumps from dependence on the wind. The huge amounts of water pumped away were moved via the locks at Spaarndam and Halfweg into the IJ estuary. The river IJ was much wider at that time and it flowed into the Zuider Zee. Use was made of the level differences of the tides in facilitating transport of pumped water. At high tide water was pumped directly into the river IJ. In order to control the water level in the Haarlemmermeer basin, one main canal and six subsidiaries crossing it were excavated, creating fields 200 metres wide and one kilometre in length. Once reclaimed, the land provided 18.539 hectares of fertile ground at one stroke.

The highly symmetrical facade of the engine house at Lynden is a typical example of utility architecture of the midnineteenth century.

This print illustrates the three stages of reclamation. At the top, the lake at the time of the relief of Leiden in 1573 is shown in the centre the pumping engine and at the bottom the reclaimed land.

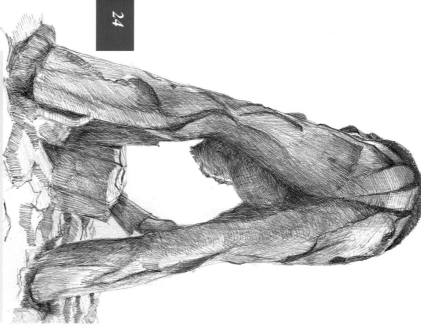

A viewing tower marks the spot where on the 28th May 1932 the last gap in the enclosing dam was filled. The nameless legion of workers who laid the millions of basalt blocks by hand to protect the flanks of the dam is honoured in a piece of sculpture.

The IJsselmeer polders

In the 17th century, just as in the case of the Haarlem Lake, plans already existed to separate the Zuider Zee from the North Sea. The conflicts of interest however were too great for the plans to be implemented. As is so often the case in history, there had to be a catastrophe first, before a safer situation could be created.

That occurred in 1916 when Waterland and the Anna Palowna polder were inundated. It was then decided to implement engineer Lely's plan to build a dam closing off the mouth of the bay and connecting the provinces of Holland and Friesland. The enclosing dam would not only be a protection against storms but would also help to reduce the silting of areas bordering the Zuiderzee. As a result of fresh water flowing in via the river IJssel there would be a buildup in the number of fresh-water basins.

Although Holland was a neutral country, the First World War did demonstrate its dependence on other countries for food supply. Between the two world wars there was a marked increase in population. Newly created agricultural land would be of great significance. According to the plans the Wieringermeer was the first lake to be drained, and three more polders followed after this.

TEXEL

WADDENZEE

Den Helder

Leemans gemaal

WIERINGER MEER POLDER 1927-1930 20.000 HA

Lely gemaal

Afsluitdijk 1927 1932

Medemblik

IJSSEL ME

Enkhuizen

NOORD-HOLLAND

Alkmaar

Hoorn

MARKERMEER

Purmerend

Amsterdam

De Blocq van Ka gemaal

Almere

ZUI 195 430

Hilversum

Baarn

Huizen

In 1926 the Zuiderzee Development Board was set up. In 1927 a 40 km2 experimental polder was drained near Andijk. Three years later the Wieringermeer polder was completed. This served as a model for the Noord-oost-polder and Flevoland. The creation of the Noordoost-polder (1937-1942) released 48.000 hectares of fertile land. When Flevoland was completed (1950-1967) another 97.000 hectares became available for agriculture, nature reserves, recreation and urban expansion. In 1990, the cabinet decided to rescind a previous

decision to go ahead with the Markerwaard polder. Today the Markerwaard is an important reservoir for drinking water. In the encircling dikes there are pumping stations that transfer excess water from the polders into the IJsselmeer. The pumping station "de Block van Kuffeler" at Almere has a capacity of 3000 m3 a minute. This would fill a row of 3 million lemonade bottles stretching for 300 kilometres every minute. The IJsselmeer basin is also very important as a shipping route, and for water recreation.

Draining of the Noordoostpolder left the island of Schokland high and dry.

Large successful farms were established on the fertile clay soil of the polders

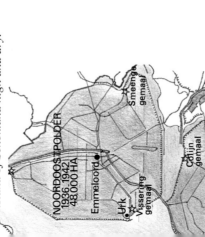

NOORDOOSTPOLDER
1936-1942
48.000 HA

Emmeloord

Urk

Vissering-
gemaal

Smeenge
gemaal

Colijn
gemaal

OOSTELIJK FLEVOLAND
1950-1957
54.000 HA

...LAND

...vink
gemaal

Harderwijk

GELDERLAND

KEY:

☐ Saltwater

☐ Freshwater

★ Pumping stations

⊥ Canals

3 PUMPING MACHINES

Early in the history of the Netherlands, excess water could only be got rid of by utilising the tidal movements of the sea. The water was released at low tide. With the introduction of windmills and later steam engines, it was possible to actively control water levels and drain land completely. Nowadays electric and diesel driven pumps do the work.

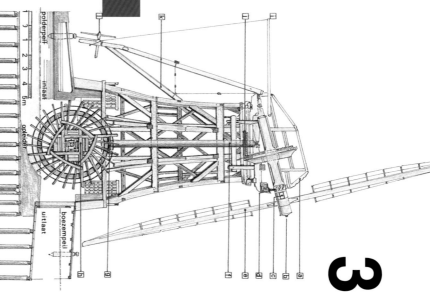

Windmills

Fortunately, the windmill is still a striking feature in the flat polder landscape of Holland. It has played a crucial role in keeping the country well-drained in its historical struggle with its archenemy, the sea. More than half of the land area lies below sea level. For every ten inhabitants of the Netherlands, six live below sea level. In the absence of dikes, water would have free reign. Continuous is pumping essential to keep Dutch feet dry.

Wind driven watermills Date from the beginning of the 15th century. The most important part is the sails. They are at right angles to form a cross and are mounted on wooden latticework on a spar. The cap of the mill together with the sails can be turned to make full use of the prevailing wind.

KEY:

a. Turning cap	g. Lower cog wheel
b. Upper axle	h. Water wheel
c. Connecting pin	i. Vane
d. Sliding bearing	j. Upper cog wheel
e. Vane	k. Tail
f. King post	l. Capstan

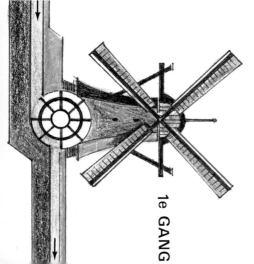

1e GANG

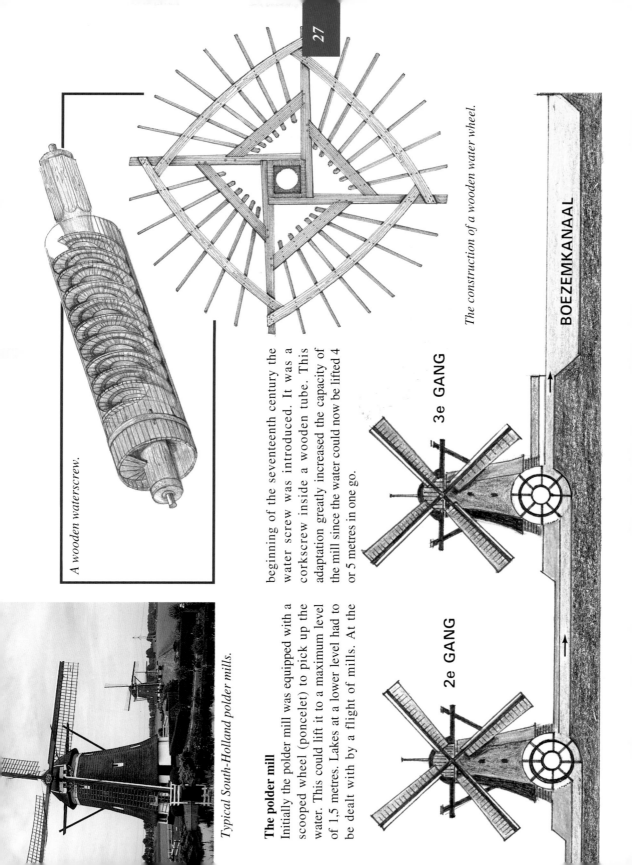

A wooden waterscrew.

The construction of a wooden water wheel.

Typical South-Holland polder mills.

BOEZEMKANAAL

3e GANG

2e GANG

The polder mill

Initially the polder mill was equipped with a scooped wheel (poncelet) to pick up the water. This could lift it to a maximum level of 1,5 metres. Lakes at a lower level had to be dealt with by a flight of mills. At the beginning of the seventeenth century the water screw was introduced. It was a corkscrew inside a wooden tube. This adaptation greatly increased the capacity of the mill since the water could now be lifted 4 or 5 metres in one go.

The group of smock mills at Kinderdijk (South-Holland) are typical polder mills.

This meant that the number of mills in a flight could be reduced - an important consideration in water management. In fact it turned out to be costly because the whole system had to be changed. Most of the poncelets were replaced by water screws during the period 1830 to 1875. The water wheel and the water screw are the most common water movers in the polder mill. The function of the water mill can only be understood in the context of water management in the Lowlands.

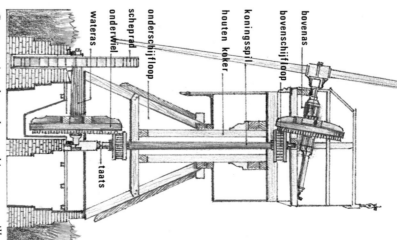

bovenas
bovenschijfloop
koningsspil
houten koker
onderschijfloop
scheprad
onderwiel
wateras
taats

Cross-section through a rocking water mill.

In a rocking mill, not just the cap, but the whole body of the mill can be turned. Although it is smaller than the smock mill the rocking mill was also used in water management. It is most common in the province of South-Holland.

Diagram of a Meadow mill.

Besides the larger types of mill, smaller versions are also to be found, for example the Tjasker in Friesland. It is an ingeniously constructed screw water mill. Another example, the meadow mill, is used for draining lowlying fields. The fan pump is usually employed in these kinds of mill.

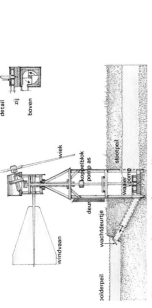

Cross section through a Boktjasker.

Meadow mill in North-Holland.

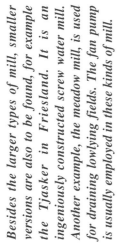

Rocking mill in South-Holland.

It is generally assumed that the rocking mill was the first to be developed, although the massive octagonal smock mill with its greater capacity was already in use before 1500. This powerful mill finally became the most common in the coastal provinces. The invention of the steam engine and the introduction of the steam pump in the middle of the 19th century signalled the end of the wind pumping era. Large numbers of polder mills disappeared. Fortunately there are still examples surviving.

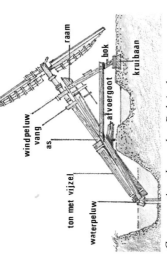

A Friesian Boktjasker.

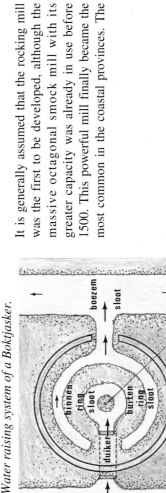

Water raising system of a Boktjasker.

The cap of the North-Holland polder mill is turned from inside so it has no "tail".

Today there are still sixty functioning polder mills in North-Holland. This could be important in times of national crisis. Because of its independence from the wind, the steam-pumping engine rapidly replaced the venerable polder mill. Application of the steam pump during the 19th and 20th centuries enabled even more ambitious projects to be tackled.

The Cruquius from an 1885 engraving. Crosssection through a steam pump.

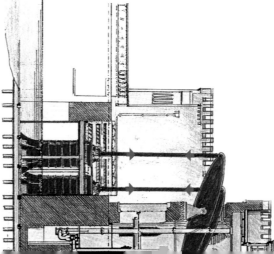

Steam pumping engine "the Cruquius"
Because the engine house of The Cruquius was built in the neogothic style, it resembles a medieval castle. Together with two other steam-pumping engines, the Leeghwater and the Lijnden, it was used to pump dry the Haarlem Lake.

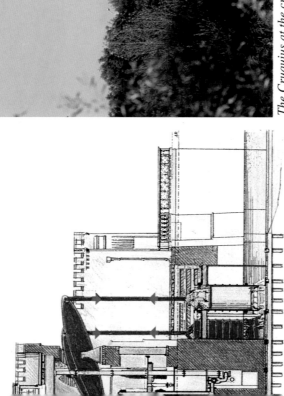

The Cruquius at the crossing of the canal with the road between Heemstede and Hoofddorp.

The Cruquius steam engine was operating from 1849 till 1933. The machinery is still intact. It was manufactured at Cornwall in England and is a socalled "Cornish Engine" working on the principle of a weigh-beam. On one side of the beam are the balance arms, on the other side the piston rods.

When the counterweight is lowered the pistons raise the water to a higher level. The piston heads have a diameter of 1,86 metres. For every revolution of the pump, they lift 8000 litres of water. Per minute of operation the engine pumps 40.000 litres of water per pump.

Detail of the engine room in the Cruquius.

There are eight pumps, so that altogether 320.000 litres of water could be lifted every minute. The water flowed from the pumps into a wooden trough running round the building. The sluices to the ring canal opened as the pressure of water built up and the water flowed into the canal and then via the river Spaarne into the river IJ and the Zuiderzee.

Modern pumps
Since 1900 the steam pumps have been gradually replaced by modern diesel and electric pumps. Even in rural areas electric pumps are now operational. Water boards have been the long established authority for water management. For example the Rhineland Water Board relies on four pump-

Modernised pumping station at Spaarndam.

The old steam pump at Halfweg pumps excess water from Rhineland into the river IJ.

A stoker at work at Halfweg.

When the pumping station was closed in 1933 it was preserved as an example of 19th century industrial technique. The building was fitted out as an educational museum of water management techniques and the Dutch system of polders.

Modern pumping station at Halfweg.

ing stations at Katwijk, Gouda, Halfweg and Spaarndam to regulate the water levels in its area. These pumps move more than fourteen million m3 of water a day. Nowadays all the pumping stations are equipped with water screws, with the exception of the one at

The Lely pumping station at Medemblik pumps excess water into the IJssel Lake.

The Rhineland pumping station at Katwijk.

These photographs of pumping stations illustrate their technical and architectural development from the preindustrial period to the clean lines of the modern functional age.

Spaarndam. This 150-year-old building has been restored to its original condition apart from the paddle wheels, which have been slightly widened. These are still in use because they are the most effective and energy-efficient way of maintain the 20 cm difference in level between water levels in Rhineland and the North Sea Canal. Modern

Modern pumping station at Alkmaar.

systems enable the pumping stations to be regulated by computer from a central control room. The water boards are also responsible for flood control on rivers and for containing seepage of seawater under the sea defences.

4

WATER AS AN ENEMY

In centuries gone by the Netherlands have been the victim of serious flooding. Fortunately hydraulic engineers are now able to build more effective defences against the everpresent threat of the sea. The rises in sea level from rivers swollen by prolonged rainfall are constant reminders of the need for these measures and for continued alertness.

It should not come as a surprise that a location by the sea at the mouth of a river delta has its dangers. It is a vulnerable region that has known serious flooding in the course of its history. Danger threatens most during North westerly storm force gales. The mass of water in the North Sea backs up along the coast because its flow is constricted in the narrow English Channel.

The combination of storm and spring tide is the worst case scenario. In the past these Northwest storms have taken their toll. Zeeland has always been a province at risk because once seawater had squeezed its way through the coastal gaps, it was trapped and could not return. The sea regularly broke through the dikes of the other coastal provinces too.

An impression of the St. Anthonisdijk breach on 5th March 1653 near Amsterdam (Etching by B.Picart, 1728)

Medieval floods

In the flood of 19th November 1248 the provinces of North and South-Holland were hit badly. The dike between Harger and Schagen was washed away in several places.

There are many illustrations depicting floods. Photography has recorded the consequences of such disasters.

In Delft even sea fish have swum through the streets. A generation later, on 14th December 1287 to be precise, the provinces of Groningen, Friesland and Zeeland were the subject of serious flooding. The notorious St.Elisabeth flood of 18th November 1421 was the result of a fatal combination of high tide and a westerly storm force gale. It caused the Groote Waard between Heusden and Putten to be flooded and whole villages and towns were washed away. Today's Biesbosch is a reminder of this disaster. During the same storm, the North-Holland dunes were breached at Petten, totally obliterating the original village. A century later, in 1530, the St.Felix flood in Zeeland breached the Westkapel defences on Walcheren and the town Reimerswaal on

Reimerswaal before and after the floods of 1634 (Atlas Van Stolk, Rotterdam).

Zuid Beverland was inundated. But the sea was still not satisfied. Two years later Zeeland was under attack again. This time the islands of Schouwen and Tholen were badly hit and North Beveland was completely inundated.

Sixteenth and seventeenth century floods

On 1st November 1570, the North-Holland coastal villages of Petten, Callantsoog and Huisduinen were flooded to a level almost 4 meters above Amsterdam mean sea level. This catastrophic flood on All-Saints day laid waste to large areas of North and South-Holland, including Amstelland, Gooiland and Rhineland.

At the same time in Friesland hundreds of inhabitants are reported to have been lost under the floodwaters. In Zeeland the "Land of Seaftinge" was washed away in a single flood.

In 1631 the town of Reimerswaal was again inundated, this time because of neglecting of the dikes. It had to be abandoned by the inhabitants. The heraldry of the province of Zeeland includes a lion emerging from the water and the motto "Luctor et Emergo" (I wrestle and prevail), which fittingly symbolises the struggle for survival. The repeated awareness. Added pattern of such natural disasters must have left its mark on the Dutch people's historical to this in the early days was the conviction that such disasters were a "scourge from God" to punish the people for their licentious way of life.

This review would not be complete without mentioning the flood of 1675. This was already a difficult period of the occupation of Holland by the French in 1672. Initially water was an ally since use was made of the "Holland Water Line" defence. But on 4th November 1675, the role was reversed and

...ght van Egmont op Zee zuytwaarts op t Strant kort na de Storm van Kers-mis a 171...

These two historical prints of Egmond on-Sea show how the sea gradually encroached on the village as a result of constant erosion of the dunes, finally claiming the tower of the church in 1717. (anonymous 18th century engraving).

a heavy storm beat on the dikes at Den Helder, inundating part of Huisduinen. The dike at Halfweg, between Haarlem and Amsterdam, collapsed under the pressure of the storm-driven water of the river IJ.

In Amsterdam the floodwater even reached the Dam in the heart of the city. On the Zuiderzee the Muider dike was breached and the towns of Naarden, Muiden and Weesp were inundated. The worst hit area was West-Friesland where the ring dike at Scharwoude collapsed leading to flooding of a wide area. The fact that breaching of dikes led to such extensive flooding in the past is a direct result of the subsidence of the land following drainage and drying out. Not only did the floods cause loss of life among both humans and animals, but also inundation by salt water rendered the land infertile for an extended period afterwards. On 22nd and 23rd November 1686, Groningen and Friesland were again seriously hit by flooding. In Groningen alone 1558 people were drowned.

Floods in the 18th and 19th centuries

Once again, on 25th December 1715, the province of Groningen was hit by floods. To make matters worse, all around the Zuiderzee, dikes were breached. Hardly a year later, on 14th and 15th November, North and South-Holland were affected. A week later there were more emergencies

The Kattenburgerplein in Amsterdam flooded in 1775 (Engraving H.Kobell by N.van de Meer).

A poem about the Haarlem Lake.

Breached dike at Durgerdam in the 16th centur...

Flooding at Monnickendam in 1916.

Cause and effect play a decisive role in flood disasters. A direct result of the floods in 1916 was the decision to construct the dam closing the mouth of the Zuiderzee.

when the river defences in South-east Gelderland and Overijssel were overwhelmed.

On 15th January 1808, Zeeland was again struggling with the sea. In 1825, 22.000 hectares of fertile land in North-Holland was affected by floods as a result of the deadly combination stormspring tide. In the province of Overijssel there was again a serious flood when the sea and river dikes were breached in several places.

In 1894 a high tide threatened the Dutch coast. There were numerous breaches of dikes on the South-Holland islands, and the resulting floods were disastrous for the inhabitants and their cattle.

Floods in the twentieth century.

In 1906 the Zeeland islands were affected when the polder between the Wester- and Ooster Schelde estuaries was inundated.

On 13th January 1916, during the First World War, there was large scale flooding in the area around the Zuiderzee. Once again North-Holland was plagued by dike breaches. In the first quarter of the twentieth century, the government finally decided to go ahead with the construction of a dam across the mouth of the Zuiderzee.

(Anonymous artist).

The 1953 flood disaster.

This disaster is grafted deep in the minds of many older Dutch people. On the 31st January 1953 a storm approaching from the sea grew to hurricane proportions. At some places the waves, driven by the storm and swelled by the high tide, raised the sea level to 4.55 metres above N.A.P. The dikes were not capable of withstanding these forces of nature and were breached in several places. On 1st February 1953, 145.000 hectares of fertile land were inundated, and some 300.000 inhabitants lost home and possessions and were lucky to escape alive.

The disaster cost 1853 human lives and clearly demonstrated the vulnerability of the Netherlands. Immediately work started on implementing the Delta project. The plan involved the strengthening of the dikes along the river estuaries and the raising of their height to Delta level. In their original proposals the government concentrated on strengthening the sea defences at the front door of the delta and neglected to secure the back door where the waters of the Rhine and Meuse flowed through the lowlands. There was also a reluctance to disfigure the landscape of the estuaries.

When conditions are critical, the dikes are continuously monitored.

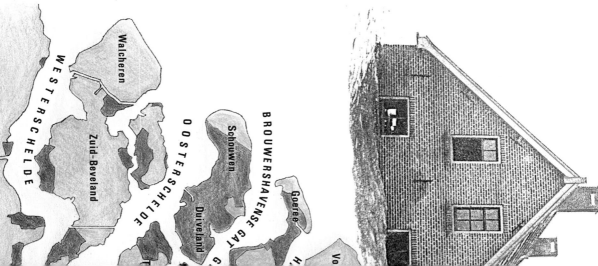

MAP OF PARTS OF SOUTHWEST
HOLLAND AFFECTED BY FLOOD
DISASTER OF 1 st FEB. 1953

Schieland   Krimpenerwaard

Alblasserwaard

elfland   Hoekse Waard

HOLLANDS DIEP

Noord - Brabant

☐ Inundated area

N

Breach in the dike at Zwingelspaan,
West Brabant, 1953.

A near-disaster in 1995

There was great concern around Christmas time in 1993 when the Meuse overflowed its banks in the South, causing serious flooding. In January 1995, the government got an even greater shock when large areas of Limburg were again inundated, and danger threatened at various locations in the delta of central Holland with dikes in a state of near collapse. For too long the dikes had been treated by successive governments as low priority, and the environmental lobby had resisted large-scale incursions in order to protect the river landscape. This combination of factors almost resulted in a catastrophe.

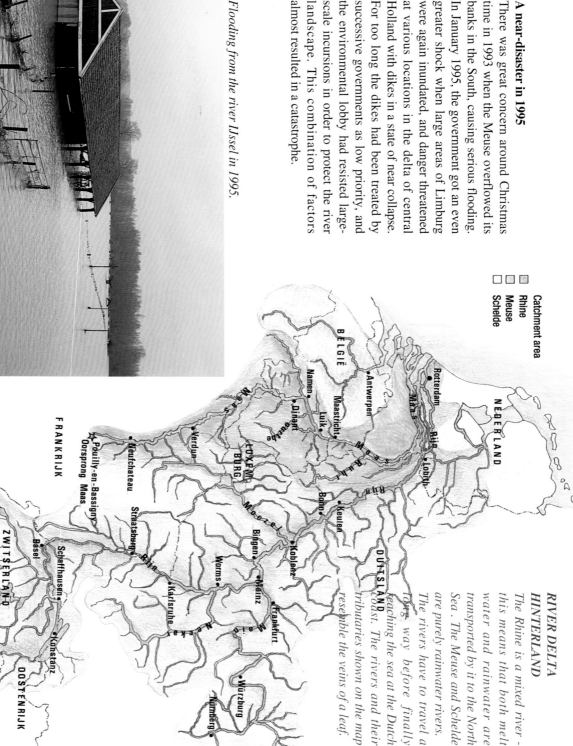

Flooding from the river IJssel in 1995.

RIVER DELTA HINTERLAND

The Rhine is a mixed river - this means that both melt water and rainwater are transported by it to the North Sea. The Meuse and Schelde are purely rainwater rivers. The rivers have to travel a long way before finally reaching the sea at the Dutch coast. The rivers and their tributaries shown on the map resemble the veins of a leaf.

Catchment area
Rhine
Meuse
Schelde

NEDERLAND
Rotterdam
Lobith
Rijn
Maas
BELGIË
Antwerpen
Namen
Maastricht
Luik
Dinant
LUXEM-BURG
Bonn
Keulen
Ourthe
DUITSLAND
Koblenz
Moezel
Bingen
Mainz
Frankfurt
Worms
Karlsruhe
Neckar
Würzburg
Nürnberg
Straatsburg
Rijn
FRANKRIJK
Verdun
Neufchateau
Pouilly-en-Bassigny
Oorsprong Maas
Schaffhausen
Basel
ZWITSERLAND
Konstanz
Schampt
Oorsprong Rijn
Felsberg
Reichenau
OOSTENRIJK

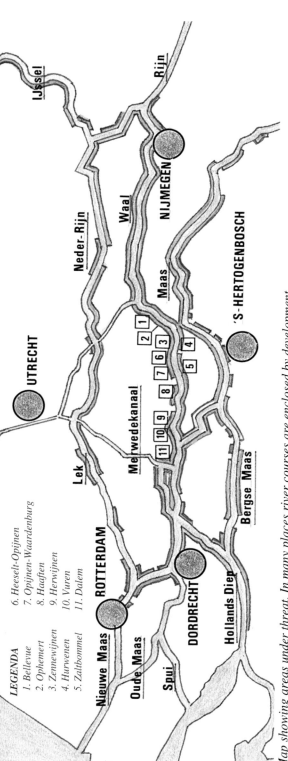

Map showing areas under threat. In many places river courses are enclosed by development.

LEGENDA
1. Bellevue
2. Ophemert
3. Zennewijnen
4. Hurwenen
5. Zaltbommel
6. Heeselt-Opijnen
7. Opijnen-Waardenburg
8. Haaften
9. Herwijnen
10. Vuren
11. Dalem

As a result of both industrialisation and urbanisation, the rivers have become extensively canalised. They have lost their capacity to absorb increases in flow and are restricted by their dikes. Over the centuries the peat marshes between the dikes have dried out to form dangerous "water bowls". In the river delta the risk of dikes being breached can never be discounted.

Government experts calculate a chance of flooding at once in 1250 years. Under pressure of circumstances emergency legislation allowed strengthening of 150 km. Of vulnerable dikes in Gelderland and Overijssel. In the year 2000 the remaining 600 km. Of old dikes were improved. The flooding of large areas of the Netherlands in the autumn of 1998, once again proves that there is a pressing need for a more flexible form of water management.

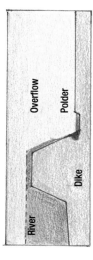

1
River
Overflow
Polder
Dike

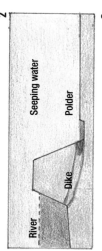

2
River
Seeping water
Polder
Dike

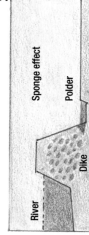

3
River
Sponge effect
Polder
Dike

Problems in water management

These can be viewed in three categories, those of the upper-, middle- and lower course of the water-flow. Each course has its own regime. On the coast (the lower course) the fluctuations of tide (twice daily), the strength of the wind (duration in days) and the peaks (duration in hours) which are capable of causing dike breaches. A breached sea dike is difficult to repair because the changing tides flush out the breach. Moreover silting renders the hinterland useless for growing crops over an extended period. It is therefore understandable that the maintenance of sea-defences has a high priority.

A different kind of problem is posed by rising water levels in the rivers of the delta (the middle course). In this case the rise in levels takes place gradually over a period of days and weeks. If flooding occurs it takes place slowly and eventually the water recedes. The regime of the middle and upper courses is of a different character to the lower course. Storage reservoirs for accommodating excess amounts of water can provide a solution. But once these are full and a further high water threatens, there is no alternative. Besides, the farmers will not take kindly to having their hard worked fields earmarked for inundation. Should this be unavoidable, then it would seem sensible to at least raise the farmstead on an artificial mound, thereby bringing the centuries old historical process full circle. With a chance of flooding on this scale once in 1250 years it is still worth considering measures like this.

Creating a flexible system

The current scientific opinion on global warming would indicate an expectation of gradual climate change. Summers will become dryer and winters wetter, and heavy downpours will become more commonplace. As a result, on infrequent occasions rivers will have to deal with increased quantities of water. Global warming causes melting at the poles resulting in a gradual rise in sea levels. The Department of Water Affairs estimates a rise of one metre during this century. Add to this the fact that the land behind the dikes is consolidating and settling, and that urbanisation is on the increase in the Netherlands, and it is impossible to avoid the conclusion that a plan of action is absolutely essential.

It is reassuring that at the start of the new millennium the Dutch government has issued a declaration of intent for the development of a 21st century water policy. The declaration has three constituents. The first is to anticipate the consequences of climate change as soon as possible. The second involves a change of attitude so that the necessity of dealing with the water problem is seen as not only applying to the downstream regions but to the upstream ones too. The third

Het Intergovernmental Panel on Climate Change heeft wereldwijde verwachtingen voor klimaatveranderingen gepresenteerd. Op basis van deze verwachtingen is een middensis van deze verwachtingen is een midden- laag en hoog scenario voor de zeespiegelstij- ging in Nederland ontwikkeld. Het lage sce- nario (A) geeft een zeespiegelstijging van 20 cm per eeuw weer, het midden scenario (B) rekent voor 2050 op 25 cm en in 2100 op 60 cm. Het hoge scenario (C) laat aan het einde van de volgende eeuw een stijging van 85 cm zien.

RIJZING IN METERS T.O.V. 1990 (bron: p. huisman)

In the matter of sea-level rising in the next hundred years are developed three scenarios.

The Krabbersgatslock at Enkhuizen between the IJsselmeer and the Markermeer. Rising water levels necessitate expensive dike raising. It is better to maintain desired water levels by enlarging the sluice capacity, although this policy has its limitations. Eventually it will be necessary to build larger pumps along the enclosing dike.

Important lock in the IJsselmeer.

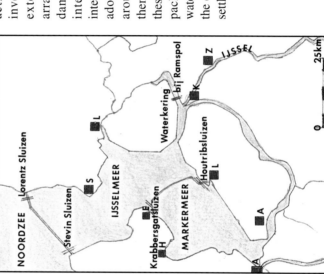

constituent involves looking for ways of creating more space for water. Measures for dealing with the contemporary water situation can be built into a "three-stage" strategy of confinement - storage - disposal. Water that can no longer be confined will have to be accommodated in retention areas until it can finally be disposed of.

During periods of excessively large quantities of incoming water, emergency overflow facilities will be needed. As a result of changed circumstances, it will also be necessary to subject all new plans for development to a "water test" in order to ensure a more waterconscious building

activity in the Netherlands. A broad investigation is needed to determine the extent to which insurance cover can be arranged for increasing amounts of flood damage. The government's declaration of intent will make it easier for various interested parties to plan for measures to be adopted on the coast, along the rivers and around the IJsselmeer, and to implement them. By 2002 it is intended to combine all these plans in a "National Policy Agreement" package, which is designed to so organise water management as to be able to deal with the expected trends in climate change, ground settlement and urbanisation.

The Ramspol bellows-barrage

In this respect the bellows-barrage between Ketelmeer and Zwarte Meer is is an interesting 21st century innovation. The unique flexible barrage is designed to protect the hinterland of West-Overijssel including the towns of Zwolle, Genemuiden, Hasselt and Zwartsluis from flooding. The installation of the barrage is intended to avoid the necessity of raising the height of tens of kilometres of river dikes. In this respect, the barrage is not only cheaper but also helps to conserve the characteristic landscape by avoiding the raising of dikes. The traditional form of barrage with its large vertically raised floodgates would also have formed a

dissonant in the landscape.

That is why Water Board Groot Salland has opted for this unusual solution. A thick roll of rubber like a huge inner tube lying on the bed of the river is the basic element of this new kind of barrage. Three giant bellows each 80 metres in length lie in a 240 metre long concrete basin at right angles to the waterway.

The barrage is automatically set in motion when the water level is half a metre higher than Amsterdam datum and is flowing in the direction of Zwolle. When this occurs a signal is sent by water meters to a central control unit. This switches on the compressors which inflate the giant eight meters diameter roll

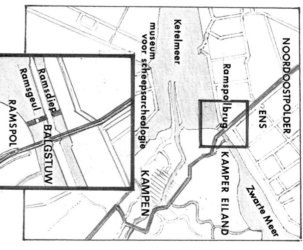

THREE STAGES OF THE BELLOWS-BARRAGE

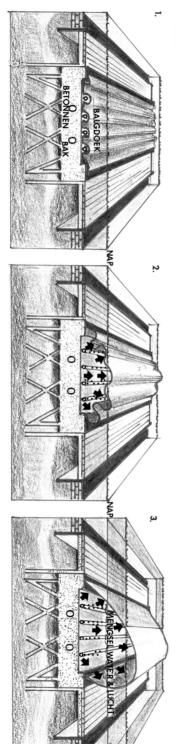

1.

BETONNEN BAK
BALGDOEK

NAP.

2.

NAP.

3.

MENGSEL WATER & LUCHT

The Ramspol barrage in operation (artists impression).

into a massive barrage.

The bellows can reach their full extent within an hour. Half full with water and air the barrier can withstand a flood level of 3,5 metres above N.A.P. The chance of such a rise in water level is estimated at once in 2000 years. Once the danger of flooding has receded, the bellows are emptied. The roll settles under its own weight (40 tons) back into the concrete basin. Because this was a totally new concept, the design engineers have applied various computer-simulated tests to the construction. This was necessary to test the barrier's reaction to fluctuations in the pressure of the waves, to extreme pressure at a single point (peaking) and to a situation where a split in the bellows occurs putting it out of action. The Technical University of Delft has recommended the application of a flexible nylonfibre sheet to the rubber roll to help it to absorb peaking and to prevent splitting. The bellows barrage is a unique construction worthy of the term "Holland's Glory".

The Ramspol barrage under construction.

Installing the rubber roll (below).

Water management in the near future

The introduction of flexible water management involves a change in thinking. It will need pioneers whose enthusiasm and professionalism provide the impetus for new projects and a vision for a modern water policy. In the coming years this new approach will have to be broadened. Through legislation and finance, the government can help to structure the process and achieve a balance between innovation and policy formulation. The final section of this chapter is devoted to a selection of innovative projects that help to illustrate how the future may be taking shape.

Dynamic coastal management has been put into practise to the North of Bergen aan Zee (de Kerf). An opening has been created in the line of sea dunes so that the sea can penetrate the dunes and create its own natural landscape. Sea defences are in no way being jeopardised.

At the expanding town of Leidsche Rijn where 30,000 houses are being built, the rainwater from roofs is led into a separate system instead of being deposited into the sewer. It is collected in "wadis" where it is allowed to accumulate and promote the growth of flora and where it naturally sinks into the ground. This is a return to earlier times when there was standing water in the winter, but now there is a system of control and there are the advantages of water storage, natural vegetation and recreation. (see illustration at the right page).

In order to increase the storage capacity in the Westland region, the Hoogheemraadschap Delfland is developing a robust bosomwater system, thus hoping to reduce the risk of flooding in this populated area of greenhouse horticulture.

The Aakvlaai polder can be looked upon as a new part of the Biesbosch. This polder of 150 hectares has been incorporated into the flood plains of the river Meuse. According to computer calculations, the Aakvlaai area will flood with river water once each year. Sacrificing the polder has given the river Meuse more space and the pressure on the dikes along the Bergsche Meuse has been considerably reduced. Positive side effects are the creation of natural landscape and more space for water recreation (see below).

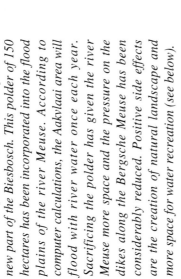

The banks of the ditches in Leidsche Rijn form part of the ecological network.

Close to the centre of Den Bosch there is an important recreation area, the Bossche Broek. With its size of 525 hectares it is one of the largest retention areas in the Netherlands, having a buffer capacity of eight million cubic metres. The construction of two concrete inlets allows optimum use of this capacity. At times of dangerously high water levels machines will dig out the bank at the location of the inlet. The site at the end of the river Dommel is marked by eight concrete posts. The chance of flooding in the streets of Den Bosch has thus been reduced by from once in a hundred years to once in a hundred and fifty. (left illustration).

5

HYDRAULIC ENGINEERING

More than half the Netherlands lies below sea level. Dikes are essential as sea- and river defences; sluices regulate the inland water levels. Bridges, tunnels aqueducts and ferries cross the waterways. They are all there in abundance.

Consolidating the dunes

At several places along the Dutch coast the dunes have been strengthened. At Petten in North-Holland the Hondsbosse seawall fills a gap in the dune. At Monster in Westland, South-Holland, the Delftland heights have been constructed to prevent erosion of the dunes, which are only 200 metres wide at this point. In Zeeland a similar measure was taken in the form of the Westkapelle sea dike at the point of Walcheren. Even today the Dutch coast is constantly changing. Man made intrusions such as the huge expanse of Europoort at the entrance to Rotterdam harbour, and the entrance piers at IJmuiden, have affected the currents along the coast.

Planting bent grass to prevent dune erosion.

Key:

1200-1600
1600-1900
1900-present

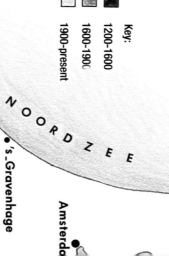

Middelborg

N O O R D Z E E

's-Gravenhage

Rotterdam

Amsterda

The dunes are essential as a protection for the hinterland and yet they are vulnerable. Dune flanks that have been washed away in a storm are often restored by pumping a mixture of water and sand up onto the dune. It is then consolidated by replanting with bent grass. The dunes are the widest at Kennemerland. At locations where the beach is very narrow, groynes have been placed to encourage beach formation. These have also been used on the South-Holland coast and on the islands of Zeeland.

Groynes on the North-Holland coast at Egmond on-Sea.

Sand is sucked up from the seabed using a pump and pipeline. The photo shows sand replenishment of the beach at Bloemendaal.

DIKES IN THE NETHERLANDS SINCE ca.1200

Groningen

Assen

Leeuwarden

Zwolle

Arnhem

genbosch

ENZEE

Workers sowing grass on the flank of a newly laid dike.

Dike building

A dike is an earthen dam designed to protect the low-lying land behind it from flooding. Its cross-section is a trapezium. The core is usually just sand or sunken caissons covered in sand and clay. The sloping flanks are covered in grass mats. In the case of sea dikes, the height of the crown of the dike is determined by the high water mark, the effects of storm winds and the advance of the wave

The statue of Lely (1854-1929) is a memorial to the hydraulic engineer and statesman who designed the plan for closing off and draining the Zuiderzee.

Cross-section of a dike which consists of:
a. toe of dike, **b.** seaward flank, **c.** the crown, **d.** inland slope, **e.** heel of dike, **f.** inner flank, **g.** dike ditch, **h.** sitting.

stone
sand
loam
h
c
clay
d
e
f
g
a
b

KEY:

☐ Dike sections, made in 1928
☐ Dike sections, made in 1929
▨ Dike sections, made in 1930
☐ Dike sections, made in 1931
☐ Dike sections, made in 1932
☐ Depth, more than 5 meter
N.A.P.

Den Oever

700 1100 1900

when they break on the flank of the dike. The crown of the dike must be set at a safe height. On the seaward side an extra layer of blocks, either basalt or concrete, are laid as strengthening. The joints between the blocks, or even the whole surface, are filled with asphalt. The toe of the dike is always submerged and is therefore covered with a layer of zinc and edge stones with a layer of loose stones on top (See page 43), which could take place at high water, would destabilise the whole structure. Holes made by moles and rats can penetrate the surface of the dike to such an extent that water attacks it from within. Prolonged highwater can transform the dike material so that it acts as a sponge and becomes liable to breaching.

Construction work started from both bridge-heads of the enclosing dike in 1927 and completion was on 28th May 1932.

View from the tower along the enclosing dike in the direction of the Friesian coast.

Kornwerd

3620

4820

3500

2000

2700

Breezand

1070

Once water has overflowed the dike it can gouge out the leeward flank and again cause breaching of the dike. If there is a lot of seepage taking place under a dike, a channel with a retaining wall can be built to collect the seepage water and so build up a pressure to counteract the seepage.

The Afsluitdijk (enclosing dam)

Completed on 28th May 1932, the enclosing dam is 30 km. in length and is made of a clay-loam mixture. In addition to its prime function of water management it also provides a direct route for road traffic to the northern towns of Leeuwarden and Groningen. The old West Friesian ring dike has become a sleeping dike no longer having to withstand the rigours of the tides,

A plaque has been placed at the foot of the viewing tower to celebrate laying the final closing section. Below is the viewing tower.

Locks

When the North Sea Canal was dug through the dunes defence at IJmuiden, a system of sea locks had to be provided to control the water level. Such facilities are to be found through-out the Netherlands wherever two waterways flowing on different levels have to be connected.

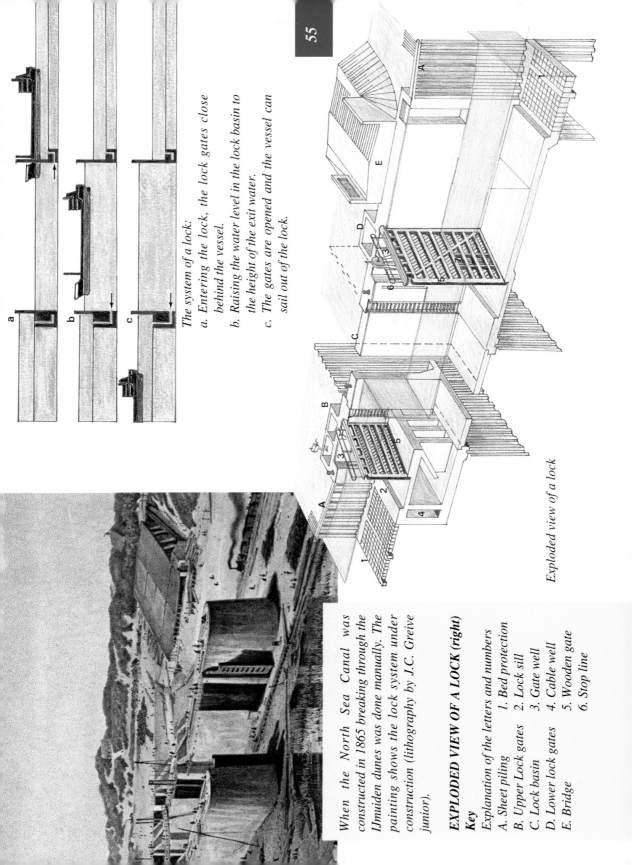

The system of a lock:

a. Entering the lock, the lock gates close behind the vessel.

b. Raising the water level in the lock basin to the height of the exit water.

c. The gates are opened and the vessel can sail out of the lock.

Exploded view of a lock

When the North Sea Canal was constructed in 1865 breaking through the IJmuiden dunes was done manually. The painting shows the lock system under construction (lithography by J.C. Greive junior).

EXPLODED VIEW OF A LOCK (right)
Key
Explanation of the letters and numbers

A. Sheet piling	1. Bed protection
B. Upper Lock gates	2. Lock sill
C. Lock basin	3. Gate well
D. Lower lock gates	4. Cable well
E. Bridge	5. Wooden gate
	6. Stop line

The sea-locks at IJmuiden.

Storm tide barrier in the Holland IJssel.

In the case of locks which connect a canal with a river or the sea where the water level outside the lock can be higher than inside, it has to be double-sided. Sea locks should always be double-sided. The large number of locks in the Netherlands is only partly related to level differences. The complicated drainage requirements inherent in the Lowlands water management system play a much greater role. The maintenance of a variety of different levels on the various inland waterways is of crucial importance. Level differences in decimetres are not uncommon.

Diagram of the most important types of locks
The lock gates turn in the horizontal plane or slide on guide rails, or they are raised and lowered in the vertical plane;

1. If the water level at the lock is alternatively high or low then double sided gates are installed.
2. The bayonet lock has a larger storage capacity.
3. A double lock with lifting gates. For ease of operation water is pumped direct from one basin to the other.

Types of lock.

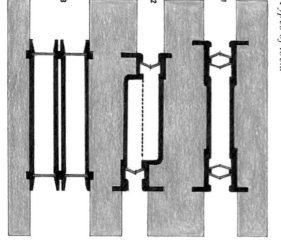

A ship encountering a difference in water levels can enter the lock when the water in the lock basin has been balanced. The process is more efficient when more ships can be handled simultaneously. In the case of sea locks an additional consideration is the large quantity of seawater entering the system every time a ship passes through and the danger of silting. Once the vessel has entered the lock, water is pumped in or out of the chamber, depending if the outside level in the destination channel is lower or higher. Then the gates are opened and the ship can then continue on its voyage.

Canalisation of rivers

In the Netherlands, shipping has always made use of natural rivers as well as manmade waterways. In the process of time measures have been taken to improve river navigability including deepening of the river bed and taking out sharp bends. This process is known as canalisation. When a bend is cut off an isolated pool remains behind the new embankment.

Other improvement measures include the placing of groynes and breakwaters in the river channel to keep it on its course. This is known as river normalisation.

Raising and strengthening a river bank.

Cross-section of a river bed.

dike   **Flood plane**   **Summerdike with groynes**   **Winter level**   **Summer level**   **Notchdike with groynes**

The water level in the rivers Rhine, Waal, Meuse and IJssel is largely dependent on the quantity of melt- and rainwater generated in the hinterland. A weir or barrier can control the water level and avoid large fluctuations. To allow the passage of river traffic a lock is necessary adjacent to the barrier and this causes delay. The Meuse is extensively canalised, and there are seven barriers on the total length passing through Holland.

The distribution of water in the delta

The river Rhine enters the Netherlands at Spijk on the German border. According to the latest figures, 8208 m3 of water a second pass through the Pannerdens Canal. The Nederrijn takes 4661 m3 and the IJssel another 3547 m3. The river Waal handles the lion's share with 11.792 m3 a second. It is the most important shipping route to Rotterdam and thus the most significant inland waterway.

River water management

The canalisation of the delta rivers together with the Zuiderzee and Delta works have created water management on a national scale. The modernisation of the rivers has transformed them into mass transport waterways. The situation in the Netherlands is special in that the interests of inland shipping has to be

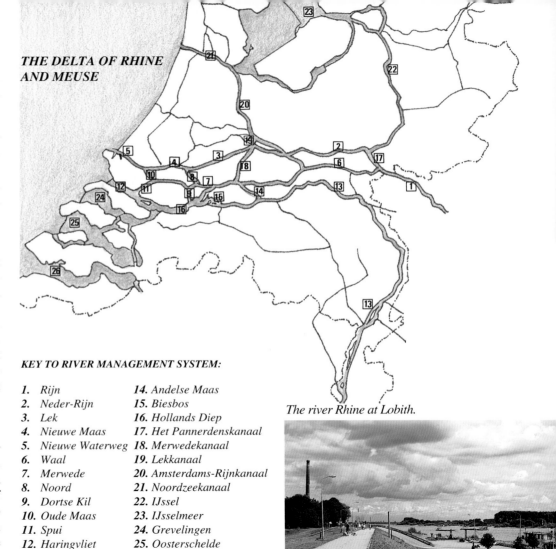

THE DELTA OF RHINE AND MEUSE

KEY TO RIVER MANAGEMENT SYSTEM:

1. Rijn	14. Andelse Maas
2. Neder-Rijn	15. Biesbos
3. Lek	16. Hollands Diep
4. Nieuwe Maas	17. Het Pannerdenskanaal
5. Nieuwe Waterweg	18. Merwedekanaal
6. Waal	19. Lekkanaal
7. Merwede	20. Amsterdams-Rijnkanaal
8. Noord	21. Noordzeekanaal
9. Dortse Kil	22. IJssel
10. Oude Maas	23. IJsselmeer
11. Spui	24. Grevelingen
12. Haringvliet	25. Oosterschelde
13. Maas	26. Westerschelde

The river Rhine at Lobith.

58

Barrier at Hagestein (1958) on the Lek in the open position. Together with the barriers at Maurik (1966) and Driel (1970) it controls the water level in the Rhine for the benefit of shipping. Annually there are 15.000 freighters and 9000 pleasure boats passing these barriers. Because the river is canalised the shipping encounters less current than on the Waal. The barriers are controlled by computer. The water level is checked every hour and if necessary adjustment is carried out. Under normal conditions the barriers are open. When the level drops to less than 11,4 metres below N.A.P. then they become operational.

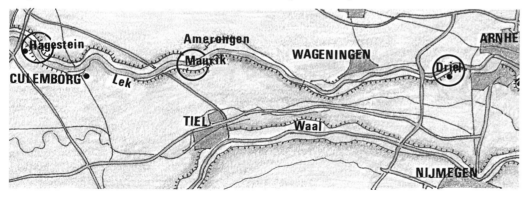

weighed against those of flood prevention. The river Rhine is a sweet water river and is not only important for shipping but also for drinking water. The barrage at Driel acts like a tap in the system and is designed to keep the IJssel navigable as well as acting as a safety valve at times of high water.

River management in the future

There is a growing conviction within the government Ministry State of Water Affairs that plans currently being formulated will have to take into account a general future rise in sea level. In general expected climate change will increase the frequency of flash flooding in the near future. To deal with these changing circumstances, the rivers' natural capacity for adjustment will have to be restored, and a more flexible river strategy will have to be adopted. As a result, the IJssel will be given an even more important role to play as a valve in the water management system.

In the 21st century it is important that sufficient guarantees can be given for the safety of those living and working in the delta. This can be achieved not only by a dike strengthening programme, but more so through an increasing awareness that the rivers must be given the room they need to accommodate varying levels of discharge.

The delta scheme

The plan for protecting the delta had already been drawn up before the flood disaster of 1953. The aim of the plan was to close off several of the river estuaries including the Haringvliet, the Grevelingen and the Oosterschelde. The implementation of the plan was even more urgent following the 1953 disaster. By closing the estuaries the coastline to be defended would be reduced by 700 km making the maintenance economically of the sea dikes much easier.

The plan involved the raising in height of the dikes in anticipation of the expected rise in sea level. There were many advantages to be gained from the closure of the estuaries. Water management would be more effective and the silting of the estuaries could be reduced and sweet water reservoirs created.

As a result of the delta scheme, the isolation of the South-Holland and Zeeland islands has been overcome. The placing of the dams has made it viable to provide a new coastal highway linking in to the Randstad highway system.

The Haringvliet dam

The Haringvliet has always been the main estuary of the rivers Meuse, Rhine and Waal. The dam with its sluices allowing movement

Detail of the lock gates.

Cross-section of the Haringvlietlock.

of water in or out of the estuary was completed in 1970. This enormous complex of sluice gates plays a key role in the water management of a large part of the Netherlands. Normally the sluice gates are closed, and only at times of maximum discharge of Rhine water is this "Netherlands' stop cock" opened. In the closed situation water from the Meuse,

The N57 road over the Haringvliet.
Cross-section through the Haringvlietlock.

SIZE OF THE ZEELAND LAKES
million m3

Oosterschelde	2000	miljoen m^3
Brouwerhavense gat	600	miljoen m^3
Haringvliet	500	miljoen m^3
Grevelingen	180	miljoen m^3
Volkerak	170	miljoen m^3
Oude Maas	37	miljoen m^3

Storm flood barrier in the Oosterschelde.

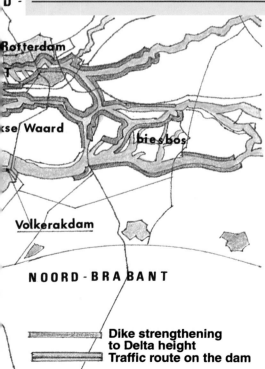

Rotterdam

se Waard

biesbos

Volkerakdam

NOORD - BRABANT

**Dike strengthening
to Delta height
Traffic route on the dam**

Waal and Lek is forced to flow into the Nieuwe Waterweg to reach the North Sea. Closing the Haringvliet has also resolved the large tidal fluctuations. The 4,5 km. long Haringvliet dam connects the islands of Voorne and Goeree-Overflakkee, and its main function is to protect the hinterland against stormtides. It took 15 years to build. There are both sluices and locks incorporated in the design, the latter providing an outlet to the sea for the fishing fleet based at Stellendam. To prevent silting the sluices are closed every high tide. During gales the dam presents a closed front to the sea.

Exploded view of the storm flood barrier.

The gates in the storm flood barrier are 43 metres wide and weigh more than 300 tons. The gates between the columns can be lowered down to threshold level.

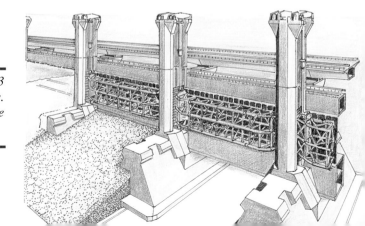

Oosterschelde barrier

the Oosterschelde estuary, like the Wadden Zee, acts as a nursery for a variety of fish species which populate the North Sea. There was such an outcry from environmental groups against plans to close off the estuary with the resulting loss of tidal regimes and salt water species such as shellfish, that the government was forced to reconsider.

In 1976 the Ministry engineers were instructed to design a moveable barrier at the estuary mouth.

Further to the East, the Philips dam in the Volkerak, and the Oosterdam between Tholen and Zuid-Beveland were placed to limit the effects of the tides and the inflow of salt water. This is called compartmentalisation.

Highway on the Ooster-Schelde barrier.

Flood barrier in the Nieuwe Waterweg.

An added advantage of the Delta scheme for shipping is that an inland waterway route free from tidal effects has thus been created between Rotterdam and Antwerp. In order to facilitate closure of the 8km. wide mouth of the estuary, three construction islands were constructed on the sandbars at Neeltje Jans, Noord-land and Roggenplaat, and provided with three dam segments totalling 5 km. in length. A dam with sixty-two retractable floodgates which became operational in 1986 controls the main channel. These gates are open in normal weather and closed in storm conditions or when the sea level rises to 3,25 metres above N.A.P. To keep the system in optimum condition each gate is closed once a month and the complete set is lowered each year in September closing the estuary completely. This is done at the turning point of the tide so as to minimise the effect on the environment. The effect of the dam has been to reduce the length of seacoast between West-Kapelle and the western point of Goeree from 800 km. to 80 km. Moreover the dam provides a direct route to the Zeeland capital, Middelburg.

The flood tidal barrier in the Nieuwe Waterweg

This is the last link in the chain of sea defences that constitute the Delta scheme. As keystone in the total concept it represents one of the most impressive achievements in hydraulic engineering for which the Dutch

At the end of the 20th century a change in emphasis is apparent in considering the Delta scheme a safety or an environmental measure. Some experts even question the need at all for the Oosterschelde barrier. By raising the level of the dikes, a lot of money could have been saved. Every year since its construction a number of sandbars have disappeared causing a scarcity in the availability of this material. New solutions are needed to solve this problem. The Haringvliet dam is currently kept partially open in order to facilitate the flow of the Meuse and avoid silting up of the river channel. This reduces the amount of dredging needed in the channel.

Detail of the latticework arm.

The flood tidal barrier at sunset.

are renowned throughout the world. At times of crisis the enormous barrier must protect the Nieuwe Waterweg and thus the harbours of Rotterdam and its hinterland from flooding. It is activated when the sea level reaches 3,20 metres above N.A.P. In this final phase of the Delta scheme, the engineers were confronted by an apparent clash of interests.

The Nieuwe Waterweg is after all economically the most important transport link in the whole of the Netherlands. On the one hand the vast amounts of shipping passing in and out of the waterway must be able to do so unobstructed. On the other hand the banks on either side of the canal would have to be raised in height considerably and over a long distance. The finally adopted solution is a moveable barrier on the scale of the Eiffel Tower in Paris.

KEY:
1. Flood gate
2. Canal bed protection threshold blocks
3. Flood gate parking dock
4. Parking dock abutment
5. Control centre
6. Ball hinge and foundation
7. Guiding tower

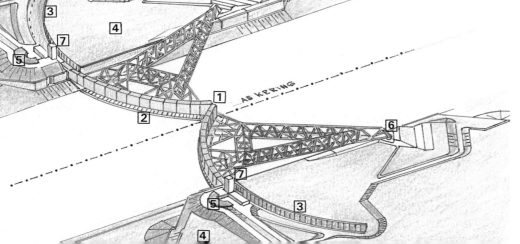

Bridges

It will come as no surprise that in the Netherlands with all its waterways there are all kinds of bridges. This wealth of variety is evident in bridges of all shapes and sizes. The building of bridges has had to keep pace with the increase in road traffic. It

Double drawbridge - Spaarne, Haarlem.

A lifting bridge "the Hef" at Rotterdam.

64

A wooden footbridge in Archeon.

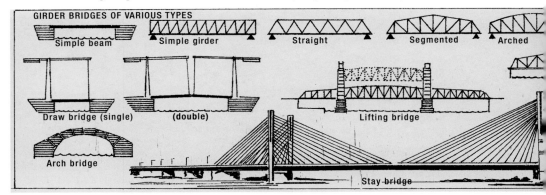

GIRDER BRIDGES OF VARIOUS TYPES

Simple beam   Simple girder   Straight   Segmented   Arched

Draw bridge (single)   (double)   Lifting bridge

Arch bridge   Stay bridge

A bascule bridge at Lemmer.

would be impossible to review all bridges of interest here, but it is useful to be able to recognise the various types and therefore diagrams and descriptions have been included. Depending on the nature of the traffic to be carried, bridges can be classified as footbridges, ordinary traffic bridges, railway bridges or aqueducts. The aqueduct is a very old form of bridge, being employed by the Romans as part of their water distribution system. Today the aqueduct is more generally applied to allow traffic to pass under a waterway. It is technically feasible to make the aqueduct

parallel variations

Suspension bridge

Bascule   and Rolling bridge

Floating bridge

65

An aqueduct.

The design of a bridge is not only a technical exercise but also an aesthetic challenge for designers. This historical review of bridge types illustrates the evolution of design and materials.

watertight and the application of this technique avoids the visual intrusion of a high bridge into the landscape.

Many of the bridges in the Netherlands are moving bridges to allow shipping to pass through. Provision of a high bridge with long inclined approaches is not only visually intrusive but also a costly investment and can only be justified in cases of economically important traffic routes. Many important bridges are impressive feats of design. In the past wood and stone were employed as building materials. Later iron and steel, reinforced

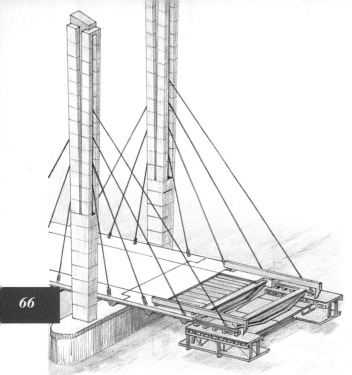

The new bridge over the Waal at Zaltbommel was built using a modern floating section method. The bridge is hung from four tall columns founded on two enormous concrete abutments 6 metres thick, 42 metres wide and 12,5 metres deep. These abutments rest on 28 concrete piles. The stay bridge is 408 metres long, 38,84 metres wide and its weight including the road surface is 23.000.000 kilograms. The headway under the bridge is 9,15 metres.

and prestressed concrete became more common materials. The various types of bridge structure can be classified as: girder arch- and suspension bridges and various types of moving bridges and also floating bridges. The design of a bridge is not only a technical exercise but also an aesthetic one. This review of bridge types illustrates the evolution of design and materials. The placing of cofferdams in the channel allows the use of shorter spans. When steel girder bridges were first introduced, spans of 150 metres could easily be achieved. With the advent of reinforced concrete, spans could be increased to 250 metres. The largest spans are to be achieved by using suspension bridges. The most striking examples in Holland are at Rotterdam and Zaltbommel.

The new stay bridge at Zaltbommel.

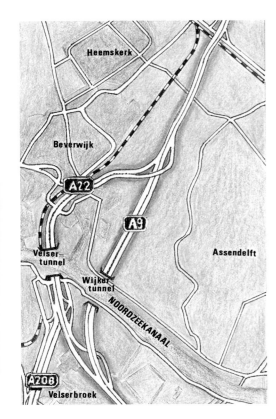

The Wijkertunnel has solved the traffic queues in the Velser tunnel. Unfortunately the problem shifts to the junction of the two highways nearby (see map).

The new Wijkertunnel helps to make an end to the congestions around the North Sea Canal.

Tunnels

The best technical solution for a river crossing is to build a tunnel., but it is also the most expensive. Even so this is often the chosen option. A fixed bridge solution has to take account of the headway required by shipping. To achieve his in the case of seagoing vessels requires an expensive bridge of enormous proportions. The alternative is a moving bridge which presents a problem for traffic with resulting tailbacks and economic effects when the bridge is open. As a consequence a city like Rotterdam has built several tunnels to ensure that shipping presents a minimum of disruption to road traffic. The same is the case in Amsterdam.

The North Sea Canal is a serious barrier for traffic in North Holland. For this reason a second tunnel, the Wijkertunnel, has been built to complement the existing Velser tunnel for road traffic passing under the canal. Hopefully this will reduce rush-hour congestion. Although the construction of such tunnels is not a problem technically, a growing awareness of the traffic implications shows that new tunnels simply generate new traffic flows. The question arises as to the wisdom of sustaining highway provision in the urbanised region of the Randstad. For several years now a dramatic improvement of public transport has been promoted to reduce journeys by car for the sake of the environment. The coming decade will have to provide an effective solution for this dilemma.

6 | WATER MANAGEMENT

Water management in the Netherlands is the responsibility of the Ministry of water affairs, provincial, local authorities and water boards. On a regional and local level, the water boards deal with water management and defences, water quality, silting & pollution prevention, and (sometimes) waterways.

The water levels differ throughout the Netherlands. Since 1885 they are all related to the N.A.P.(Normal Amsterdam level). This was established in 1675 by burgomaster Hudde of Amsterdam when he introduced a coherent system of measuring levels related to a common datum. Large parts of the Netherlands lie below N.A.P.

The water boards

The continuing necessity to keep the water at bay has contributed in no small measure to the awareness in Holland of the importance of communal welfare. The first community organisations were the rural hamlets. They looked after the common interests of the local population including the task of water management. Later a new form of organisation was needed to effectively manage water defence on a larger scale. In the twelfth century the water boards were created. The cost of maintaining the ditches and dikes, riverbanks and the quayside walls and roads were financed by the owners of adjacent farms and estates. The tenants of the estate were levied to raise the estate contribution. The inhabitants of the farms were also responsible for ensuring that their land was

The colourful heraldry of the ancient water boards illustrate their varied histories, some of which can be traced back into the medieval period.

A water board by-law from 1734.

MANAGEMENT STRUCTURE OF A WATER BOARD

Various interest groups are represented on the governing body. The board exercises the principle: interested party, contribution, representation. The degree of involvement is directly related to the degree of interest.

- ◗ *Residents (inhabitants)*
- ◗ *Owners of real estate*
- ◗ *Owners of land*
- ◗ *Users creating effluent*

drained properly. The dike-reeve and his officials ran the water board. The position of dike reeve can be compared to that of burgomaster. The mandate of the board was to ensure that the tenants of the land were carrying out their water defence commitments.

The present day water boards

By the beginning of the 19th century, a widespread system of water regulation rights had been established but its nature was inconsistent. The constitution of local and regional governing boards varied greatly depending on the local situation. In 1993 a constitutional change was introduced designed to establish conformity among the water boards. The boards were given the same legal status as a local authority. The provinces were mandated to create new boards and to abolish existing ones as required, and to administer their activities. The board itself is authorised to draw up regulations stipulating the duties of the residents of within its area. Sanctions are included for failure to abide by these ordinances (historically known as by-laws). The dike-reeve remains the figurehead of the water board. This management function is exercised in collaboration with the elected members of the "Hoogheemraad". Apart from the enforcement of water management regulations, the board is also concerned nowadays with landscape management of the dikes and their flora and fauna. Water quality and pollution levels of surface water are another of their concerns.

Ditch maintenance

Ditches have to be kept clear to allow the drainage of excess water from the bosom.

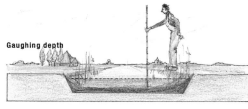

Gaughing depth

Dredging by hand

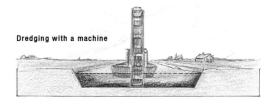

Dredging with a machine

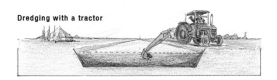

Dredging with a tractor

The bosom water

For areas that have been drained and reclaimed, the bosom is a very important factor. The term bosom refers to the whole network of open water including lakes, canals and ditches. Apart from transporting water, the bosom can be used for flushing out polluted and seepage water. This water network acts as a buffer for surplus water from the low-lying polders. It can store a certain amount of water and therefore is important in times of heavy rainfall. When urbanisation increases, the storage capacity of the bosom can come under pressure. The more surface area is covered by roads and buildings, the more runoff is diverted to the polder system. The bosom pumps have to be capable of dealing with this intake quickly enough. During long dry periods, evaporation takes place and then extra water has to be imported into the system to protect the area and its vegetation from dehydration. A drop in the water level of 2cm. can cause the roots of plants to rot. The wooden foundation piles of older buildings are also vulnerable. If the groundwater level drops to expose the pile heads, they start to rot, leading to serious settling of foundations. Maintaining the correct level in the bosom is therefore essentiial for the buildings in the

DAGRAM OF WATERMANGEMENT IN THE LOW COUNTRIES

Annual precipitation .75 cm

WATERBALANCE

Sea level

Dunes

Seepage ca. 40 cm

Peat

Sand

KEY
1. *Shallow polder with ditches*
2. *Small rocking mills*
3. *Deep polder with ditches*
4. *Inland waterway*
5. *River dike*
6. *Seepage ditch*
7. *Electric pump sta*

Evaponation ca. 45cm

↑↑↑↑↑↑↑↑↑↑↑↑↑↑↑↑↑↑↑↑↑↑↑↑↑↑

O CM   [9]   [10]   [7]

[4]

[8]   [5]   [10]   [5]   [6]

O NAP

Riverclay

8. *4-stage flight of smock mills*
9. *Steam pump*
10. *Bosom water*
11. *External water*

area, for agriculture and horticulture and for shipping. The water level at which the bosom has to be maintained for the system to work is called the bosom level. In the polders this is usually below NAP.

Our drinking water

This is the responsibility of the water companies. Tap water in the Netherlands is of good quality and can be consumed without danger to health. This is a luxury too often taken for granted In southern Europe the dry conditions present a problem for drinking water. In these parts the population is used to having to buy drinking water in bottles. But even for a large city like Amsterdam, it was not until the second half of the nineteenth century that the first attempts were made to find a better system for providing drinking water.

Rainwater and water boats

It is interesting to recall how a city like Amsterdam provided its drinking water before these improvements were made. In the Middle Ages the population simply took their water from the city canals. It was safer to drink beer and this became the brew for the common people.

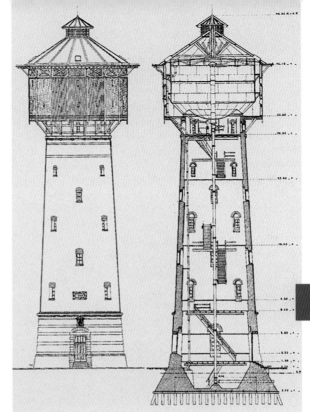

Water towers were used to provide piped drinking water at a pressure. This system s now outmoded. The towers are still landmarks in the landscape.

Diseases such as the pest, cholera and typhus were commonplace. Not until the nineteenth century was it discovered that the cause of many diseases was the impurities in the drinking water. There were alternatives. Small houses had water butts. Large houses could collect the run-off from their roofs in water tanks, a method reserved for the very rich. The city provided "fresh water" in water tanks; a relative term considering the vermin and other deposits carried off from the rooftops. The water quality was suspect and there was a risk of lead poisoning since all the water pipes were made of lead. Besides the rainwater there was the option of buying water from the waterboats. This was water brought by barge into the city from the rivers Vecht and Gein. This was still a regular trade in 1844. Due to the difficulty of manoeuvring in the river Amstel, the water was off-loaded from the barges into lighters.

About 290 lighters were distributed over the canals of the city. The water lighter had a wooden pump in the centre of the boat and the water was carried to the houses in two buckets called a "gang". One gang cost 4 cents. There was also a carrier selling water as well as milk, and these products were sometimes mixed.

Pumping station at the Oranjekom in the Amsterdam Water Company dunes.

Water lighter selling Vecht water on an Amsterdam canal.

KEY

1-5 infiltration areas
____ *collecting canals*
◄___ *normal direction of flow*
●___ *separating dam or weir*
■ *pumping station*
..... *deep wells*

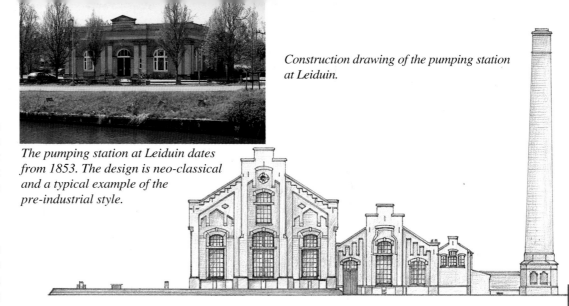

Construction drawing of the pumping station at Leiduin.

The pumping station at Leiduin dates from 1853. The design is neo-classical and a typical example of the pre-industrial style.

In Amsterdam there were wells, but the water was of poorer quality than the imported water. It was discovered that water for consumption should first be boiled, but since this required extra fuel, it was to remain a privilege of the well to do.

The first Dune Water Company

This was not a state venture but the initiative of a private company. In 1851 the Thorbecke government issued the first license to a "Dune Water Company". Strangely enough this company was financed with English capital and was based in London. We can conclude that England was more advanced in developments in this field. It is also possible that the capital needed for such a venture was not available in Holland. It was not until the end of 1853 that a 23-kilometre long cast iron pipeline could be laid from the dunes at Leiduin to Amsterdam. The initial reaction of the Amsterdam citizens was one of suspicion. They felt that the water tasted "flat" and preferred their "lively" tasting water. Gradually they came to appreciate the new supply.

Between 1870 and 1890 the economic climate in Amsterdam steadily improved and the population increased by more than 50%. In 1877 second pipeline was laid. However the water abundance of the dunes was only superficial. The more there were canals dug in the dune area, the more the ground water level dropped. After 1903, fresh water was extracted from deep bells of water which had built up over the centuries under the clay level. This water was pumped up into the extraction canals on the surface.

At the close of the previous century, the city of Amsterdam had acquired the almost bankrupt Dune Water Company, and renamed it the "City Water Company".
The last major development took place during the period 1957 - 1968, when the surface filtration of pretreated river water was introduced. A pumping station capable of transferring 70 million m3 of water a year from the river Rhine to the dune area was constructed at Jutphaas on the Amsterdam Rhine Canal.

Water from the (river) Vecht and lake

Dune water is not the only kind of water used currently to supply the city of Amsterdam with drinking water. On 1st April 1889, the Vecht pipeline with a pumping station at Weesperkarspel was brought into service. The water from the river Vecht was not suitable for drinking and was intended as cleaning water for industrial use. As a result Amsterdam had two water pipeline systems. After 1930 the supply was no longer extracted from the Vecht but via seepage water from the Bethune polder, a reclaimed lake near Loosdrecht. This could be used for drinking water. In 1980 this source was also exhausted and the capacity had to be supplied from the Amsterdam-Rhine Canal.

Distribution

Following purification, the drinking water

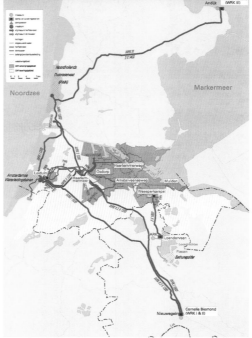

Trunk pipeline serving Amsterdam.

WATER PURIFICATION PROCESS

1. **Sources**
   The water comes from the Amsterdam-Rhine Canal and the Bethune polder.
2. **Coagulation and sedimentation**
   Iron chloride is added, pollutants coagulate and settle out.
3. **Purification tanks**
   The wind mixes the water. It stays here for 100 days.
4. **Rapid sand filtration**
   The water is drained through filter beds with layers of gravel and fine sand.
5. **Buffer reservoir**
   Variation in the rate of supply can be accommodated here.
6. **Ozonisation.**
   Ozone gas is pumped through porous ceramic pipes and mixed with the water. This improves the water quality.
7. **Softening**
   Reducing the amount of Calcium in the water.
8. **Carbon filtration**
   The carbon dioxide breaks down bacteria biologically.
9. **Flush water processing**
   A large amount of flush water (more than 90%) is returned to the purification process by means of filtration.

The process for purifying dune water is similar, only in this case the sand dunes act as a natural filter.

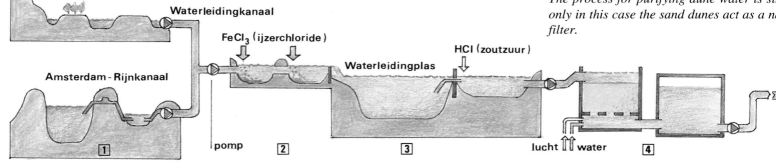

must be delivered to households and firms in and around Amsterdam. A distribution network consisting of 2000 km. of pipeline and 7 water pumps does this job at the present time. Amsterdam uses 83 million m3 of water daily. In the year 2000 this represents a daily level of consumption of 150 litres of water per person.

Privatisation?

The trend today is towards privatisation of facilities. In this respect the Amsterdam City Water Company is an interesting example since it began as a private company. The question arises as to whether the public interest can best be served by a private monopoly? A pure supply of water fulfils a basic human need, and there is a risk that profit instead of water quality and guaranteed supply, will become a more important consideration in the free market.

The water supply plant at Weesperkarspel.

10. Slow sand filtration
The water drains slowly through a bed of very fine sand.
11. Storage
The drinking water is ready for use

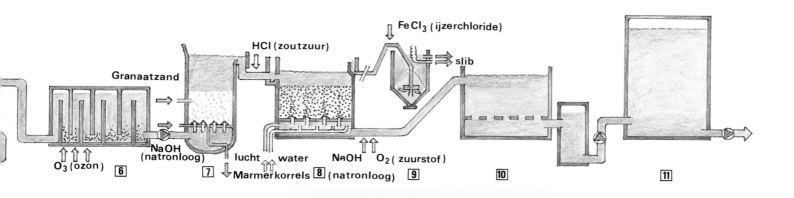

Treating sewage

Legislation to prevent the pollution of surface water has been in place since 1970. Business and households usually have a connection to the sewer system. The effluent in the sewage treatment plant undergoes a series of intensive purification processes after which it is returned to the surface water system. Untreated sewage illegally entering the system is usually easy to trace since a permit is required for the dumping of wastewater. The sewage sludge remaining at the end of the treatment process used to be returned to the land as manure. This is no longer allowed because of the risk of spreading environmentally dangerous substances. The sludge can contain heavy metals such as lead, mercury and copper from old water pipes. Other pollutants are herbicides, insecticides and manure, originating in agriculture and horticulture. Precipitation, run-off from roads, inland waterways used by shipping and landfill sites all contribute to pollution. The standard of water quality is constantly being monitored in the laboratory. They not only measure the quality of the water and of the sewage sludge, but they also check conformity with conditions attached to the license. It is clear that pollution must be dealt with at source and that pollutants must be prevented from entering wastewater. This is the only way the quality of wastewater can be consistently improved.

Checking a sample in the laboratory.

Taking a sample of water.

DIAGRAM OF A SEWAGE TREATMENT PLANT

Water boards who are responsible for the quality of wastewater have had to invest in completely new kinds of treatment plant.

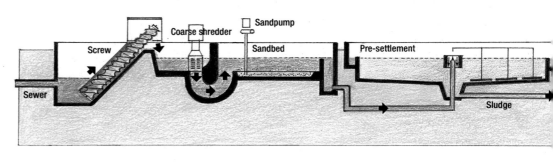

The working of a purification plant

Wastewater from industry and households is pumped to the treatment plant through the sewer. The solid waste is trapped and shredded. Heavier particles settle out in the sand bed. The water is then pumped to the settling tank where the lighter particles separate out. In the aeration tanks high-speed revolving paddles increase the oxygen content of the water. This helps the bacteria already present in the water to break down further any impurities left over. The resulting sewage sludge mixture is pumped to a final settling tank where the water is stationary. The sludge sinks to the bottom and is taken to be used as manure and as landfill. Today there are approx. 400 treatment plants which handle more than 90% of the wastewater before returning it to the environment.

77

Watertreatment plant at the Waarderpolder in Haarlem.

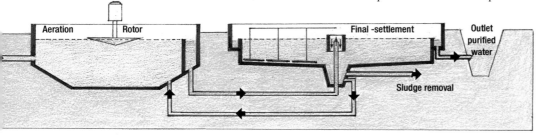

The treated water flows into a gutter at the edge of the final settling tank and is then ejected into the surface water system, thus completing the water recycling process.

7 WATER AS A MEANS OF TRANSPORT

The Netherlands' early development as a trading nation is due to its favourable location on important shipping routes. In a period that overland routes were far from comfortable, Holland had an excellent network of waterways. Many Dutch towns owe their importance and wealth to water.

The location of the Netherlands

The rapid economic development of the Low Countries is mainly due to their position on the North Sea at the mouth of the river delta. The Netherlands had a strategic location straddling the East-West trade route between the German hinterland and a developing England. The same advantage applied to the North-South trade route between Scandinavia and the countries on the Baltic Sea and the countries around the Mediterranean.

The position by the sea and the navigability of the rivers were crucial factors. The origin and wealth of many Dutch towns is due to their position on a waterway. The easily navigable Dutch inland waterways often influenced the choice of route when sailing a course on a North - South journey.

An East-Indiaman on the open sea.

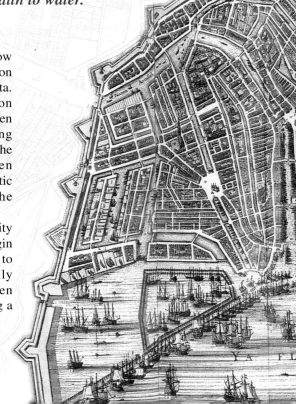

Amsterdam in the Golden Age.

Amsterdam is a trading port of international standing. It experienced a period of sustained expansion in the 17th century. This was the "Golden Age" for Holland and Amsterdam was renowned over the whole world. The growth achieved by the city at this time can still be identified in its layout and can be compared to the growth rings of a tree. The increasing wealth of the city resulted in enormous population growth and this was accommodated by the construction of an increasing number of concentric canals This example was later followed by many other towns in Holland, but nowhere as beautifully expressed as in Amsterdam.

The centurieslong familiarity with water transport within the Delta region and with sea transport outside it nurtured a rapid development of international trade. At the time of the revolt against Spanish rule, the inhabitants of the liberated provinces, enriched by the influx of Flemish refugees, began spreading their wings in the direction of the Far East. As a result of flourishing trade and successful war strategies in the seventeenth century the republic had built up an impressive trading fleet and a powerful navy. Sea transport was an important stimulus for the trading spirit of the Dutch. Through the founding of the East India Company in 1602 and subsequently the West India Company in 1621, the young republic played an increasingly dominant role in trade and Amsterdam became the staple market for the whole of Europe.

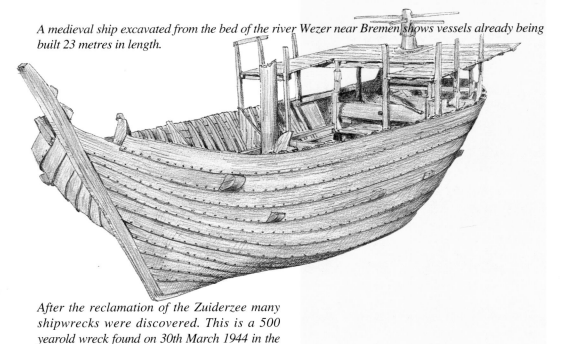

A medieval ship excavated from the bed of the river Wezer near Bremen shows vessels already being built 23 metres in length.

After the reclamation of the Zuiderzee many shipwrecks were discovered. This is a 500 yearold wreck found on 30th March 1944 in the Noordoost polder.

Inland shipping

Already in prehistoric times the settlers in this marshland environment made use of small vessels to transport men and animals. Tangible evidence of this has been found in the form of the "Pesse ship" buried in peat ground and estimated by the latest techniques to be over 6,000 years old. Prior to the coming of the Romans, the Friesians traded with Flanders, England and the regions along the river Rhine. Dorestad, Maastricht and Cologne were already important centres.

Archaeology

Finds from archaeological digs indicate that by the 7th century Dorestad had become an important trading centre. Landing jetties of considerable length found at Wijk bij Duurstede would seem to confirm this.

Dorrestad was an important centre for trade both between the Baltic and the Meuse region and between England and the German Rhineland.

The discovery of ancient charters and the excavation of old shipwrecks tell us a lot about the way inland shipping developed. Large numbers of wrecks were discovered when the Haarlem lake and Zuiderzee were reclaimed. It was also possible to investigate their cargoes and gain an insight into life on board and the ports of call. The clay bed of the lakes has conserved the vessels' remains.

Busy shipping off Enkhuizen harbour. A coloured engraving by D.de Jong, 1780

When the timbers are exposed for archaeological analysis they have to be kept moist to prevent dehydration and pulverisation. Nowadays impregnation with a plastic preservative can be applied.

Barge traffic
In the sixteenth century the busy overseas trade led to the growth of towns and this in turn created a demand for regular inland waterway connections. Regular sailing times and fixed tariffs were established.

The skippers involved in this trade were called "packet skippers" and they provided the socalled "packet services". Towns such as Amsterdam, Haarlem, Leiden, Gouda and Hoorn were connected in this way. The packet skippers had a licence and a mooring in the town harbour. The high sums required for the awarding of these licences would indicate that the trade in passengers and freight was a lucrative one.
By means of by laws all kinds of regulations were imposed on the packet skippers by the

towns they served. For instance, to ensure the safety of alighting passengers, packets were required to make fast both fore and aft. An impression of the extent of services can be gained from the fact that in 1765 there were 800 sailings from Amsterdam serving 180 destinations. By the end of the nineteenth century the system of privilege and bureau-cracy led to private initiatives.

Packet services

Travelling by road was not a pleasant ex-perience since there was no paving and after heavy rainfall the surface turned to mud. To improve the packet service canals were dug and in the seventeenth century there were regular canal services between Leiden, Haarlem and Amsterdam. The barges were towed by horses walking on towpaths alongside. At regular intervals the horses were changed, rested and groomed.

Passengers had to transfer to other barges at halfway stations. The town Halfweg between Amsterdam and Haarlem owes its name to this and in 1661 recorded 164.281 passengers changing barges at this point.

Travel by barge was popular and was noted by foreign visitors for being both cheap and comfortable.

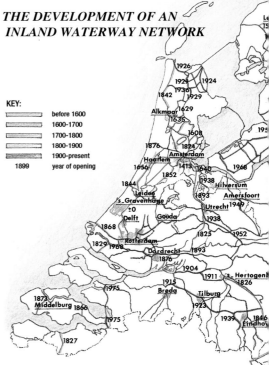

THE DEVELOPMENT OF AN INLAND WATERWAY NETWORK

KEY:

	before 1600
	1600-1700
	1700-1800
	1800-1900
	1900-present
1899	year of opening

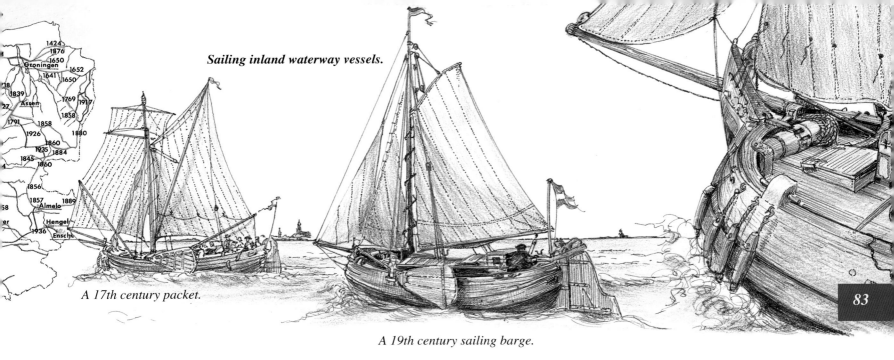

Sailing inland waterway vessels.

A 17th century packet.

A 19th century sailing barge.

Ship versus car

Paved roads first appeared in the first half of the 19th century and until this time the packet barge was the only alternative. It may seem surprising today people prefered train and tram for longer distances and took the initiative for long distance travel from paved roads. Road traffic has subsequently tipped the balance the other way. During the "First Dutch Road Conference" in 1920, measures were taken to stimulate travel by motor car.

Development of the barge

It is assumed that inland waterway craft have their origins in the Viking ship. During the period 800-1000 the Vikings threatened the coastal areas of Europe. They penetrated deep inland along the rivers. The squat built barge could be a derivative of these large open vessels which could be sailed or rowed. The flatbottomed barge is ideal for use in the shallow inland waters.

The fixed rudder made its debut in the twelfth century. The stability of the flatbottomed vessel was greatly improved by the introduction of leeboards. The sailing barge became the most common vessel in Holland and Friesland. A seagoing version of the sailing barge was also developed and vessels of several hundred tons sailed to South America and Africa. There were two types of barge, the "Tjalk" and a straightbowed "Kraak".

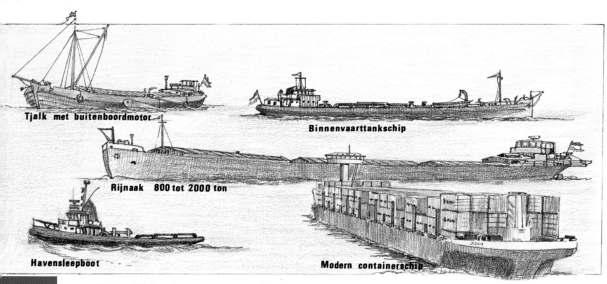

Tjalk met buitenboordmotor

Binnenvaarttankschip

Rijnaak 800 tot 2000 ton

Havensleepboot

Modern containerschip

Typical inland waterway vessels.

Inland waterway vessels near Willemstad.

The Tjalk is still in use and there are regional variations on the design.

In the second half of the nineteenth century, wooden construction began to be ousted by steel, and sail power by motor driven vessels. The sail powered barge has now passed into history. The barges plying the rivers of the delta have become floating containers. Several barges can be linked together and propelled forward by a motor unit.

Group barging
This form of transport has become increasingly common since 1957 on the inland waterways. It is a very efficient system. A powerful pushing tug can deal with several barges at once.

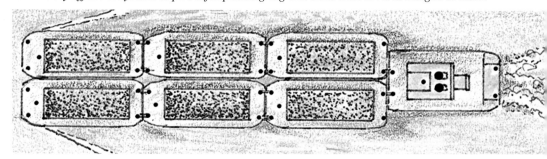

The brown fleet

Fortunately there still are a considerable number of sailing barges. The sailing tradition is kept alive at numerous locations in Holland. The skippers of these historic vessels offer various cruise arrangements of shorter or longer duration. Life and work on board these vessels can be experienced during the voyage. There is no question of mechanisation and loading and unloading take place by means of a man- operated rope and pulley. Visitors are welcome to give a hand. The skipper ensures the stability of his loaded ship which is essential for good sailing. The load must not start shifting during a storm. The skippers of these historic trading vessels join together in promoting their restoration and conservation in an association devoted to this aim. They are collectively known as "The Brown Fleet" because of the colour of their sails.

On reaching its destination, the tug can immediately transfer to another set of barges. The turn-around time and crew is reduced to a minimum.

WATERWAY TRAFFIC (*six EUR Rhine countries -in % - around the year 2000*)

Nederland	45,2%
Frankrijk	21,2%
Duitsland	19,8%
België	12,5%
Zwitserland	1,2%
Luxemburg	0,1%

Bron: CBS, NEA, VEV. (eind vorige eeuw).

The brown fleet is a picturesque sight in the harbour at Zierikzee.

85

New canal construction

In the second half of the nineteenth century the development of the economy received a stimulus from increasing industrialisation. Both sea-going and inland waterway vessels grew in size and draught.

Access to the sea for cities such as Rotterdam and Amsterdam became a problem. The Amsterdam harbour began to silt up. The following describes the measures taken by these two important cities.

A " camel" being used to move a sea-going ship across shallow water at Pampus.

The North-Holland Canal

In earlier times the seagoing ships approached Amsterdam harbour across the Zuiderzee. In adverse conditions the ships could experience delays of up to three months because of dependence on wind direction and the necessity of crossing the shallows at Pampus.

The larger vessels of the 17th century had to be carried over on "camels", a kind of floating dry dock. Den Helder lies at the tip of North Holland on the Nieuwediep.

In 1781, Willem V constructed a naval base here and during the occupation of the Netherlands by Napoleon Bonaparte the strategic importance of the town was recognised. Napoleon further fortified the town and turned it into the Gibraltar of the North.

After the departure of the French, much to the disapproval of Amsterdam, Willem I ordered the improvement of the harbour at Den Helder.

The Amsterdam city fathers were concerned about the effects on their own harbour of the resulting competition. The king however realised the need for better access to the sea, and the North-Holland Canal would provide an ideal solution to this problem.

Purmerend from the "Great North-Holland Canal", aquatint painting by H.W.Hoogkamer, 1880.

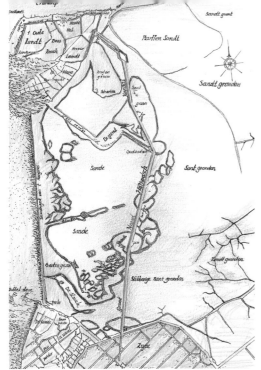

Koegras map with North-Holland Canal

View of Purmerend from the North-Holland Canal.

Reluctantly Amsterdam agreed to a proposal for the construction of a canal. There was a pressing need for a better approach to the sea. Their main motive was to win time.

A well-known military and hydraulic engineer, Jan Blanken Janszoon (1755-1838), first Inspector General in the time of Emperor Napoleon was commissioned by King Willem I to draw up a plan for creating a canal.

In 1819 construction work began in Den Helder, and in December 1824 the canal was ready for use by shipping.

The North-Holland Canal is almost 80 km long and is 37 metres wide, being able to handle ships of up to 4,9 metres draught. The designer of the canal deepened many existing waterways and the whole job took 10.000 men five years to complete.

Announcement of construction price rates.

The work was done by hand using shovel, wheelbarrow, pulley and tackle. The canal served its purpose throughout the first quarter century of its operation. During the first 25 years the Canal served its purpose very well.

Cross- section of the North- Holland Canal

Fregat Bellona
16ᵗ December 1824

Christina Bernardina
16ᵗʰ December 1824

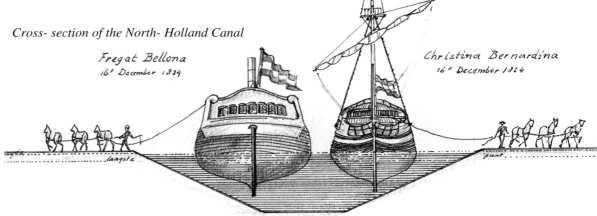

Warships in the harbour and at anchor in the Nieuwediep at Den Helder. In the background the repair yard of Willemsoord. Lithograph by A.W.van Voorden, ca.1900.

Engineer Blanken had estimated the average sailing time in favourable conditions at 15 to 16 hours and this was confirmed in practice. Increasing use was made of steam tugs to tow sailing ships through the canal. In 1884 the number of sea going ships using the canal was estimated at 1200 to 1500. After construction of the new North Sea Canal in 1865, the North-Holland Canal took on a reduced role as a route for inland waterway traffic and as a major drainage canal for this major part of North-Holland.

The North Sea Canal

This is currently the most important link for Amsterdam with the sea. The canal was constructed between 1865 and 1876 following plans by W.A. Froger. For most of its course the canal has been dug in the former bed of the river IJ but at IJmuiden it breaches the line of sea dunes. As a result of the digging of the canal, polders were

Illustration 1. St.Maartens floating bridge over the North-Holland Canal.
Illustration 2. The sea lock at IJmuiden. The North Sea Canal was opened on 1 Nov. 1876.
Illustration 3. The North Sea Canal trace.
Illustration 4. The Hembrug was an obstruction in the North Sea Canal and has now been replaced by a tunnel.
Illustration 5. The modern complex of locks at IJmuiden.

1

drained on either side of it. The 19 km-long canal has been widened to 200 meters and dredged to a total depth of 15 metres. The 3 km-long piers at the entrance protect it from silting up. In 1992 an entrance to a new yacht harbour was made in the South pier.

At IJmuiden there are are three lock systems. The 400 metres-long North Lock dating from 1930 is one of the largest in the world. On the Eastern side of Amsterdam, the Oranje Lock connects with the IJsselmeer. In this way the Amsterdam harbour forms one large dock. The digging of the North Sea Canal was a determining factor for the continued economic growth of the city in the last quarter of the nineteenth century.

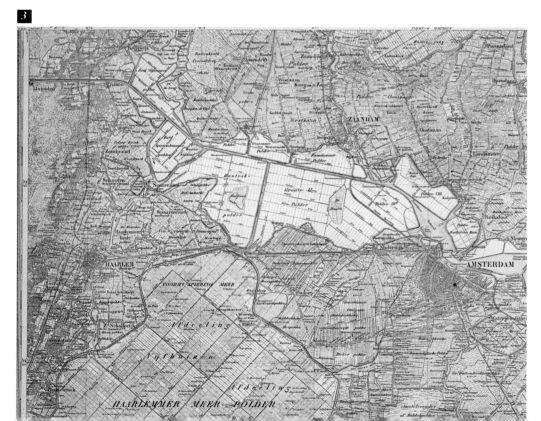

89

5

The IJmond

The possibility of introducing an additional larger sea lock into the system at IJmond is currently being investigated. Such a facility would greatly improve the accessibility of the harbours served and stimulate the regional economy. Large beamed ships would then be able to reach the harbours of Amsterdam, Beverwijk, IJmuiden and Zaanstad. This development would bring large-scale intrusion and the consequent loss of landscape value in the region.

Amsterdam is the second most important port of the Netherlands. It has a direct connection to the North Sea via the North Sea Canal. 4000 ships use the port facilities every year.

Artist's impression of the introduction of an extra lock in the system at IJmuiden.

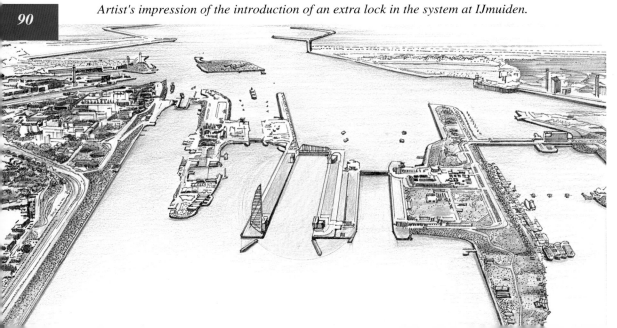

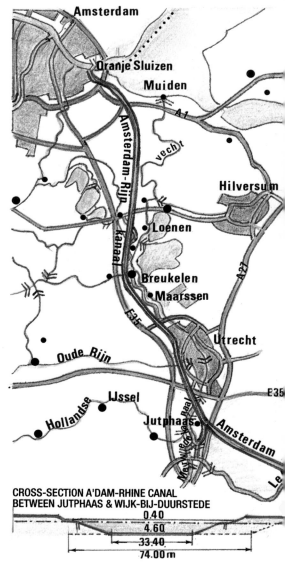

CROSS-SECTION A'DAM-RHINE CANAL BETWEEN JUTPHAAS & WIJK-BIJ-DUURSTEDE
0.40
4.60
33.40
74.00 m

AMSTERDAM-RHINE CANAL CROSSING THE RIVER LEK

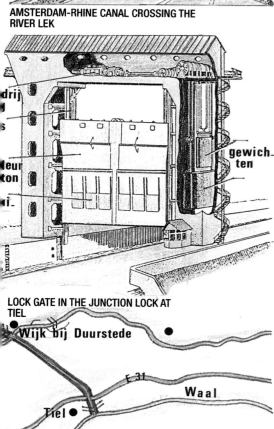

LOCK GATE IN THE JUNCTION LOCK AT TIEL

The Amsterdam-Rhine Canal

Amsterdam skippers were already sailing up the Rhine to Cologne and even as far as Basle in the year 1400. They transported beer and grain from Hamburg and timber from Norway, and returned with Rhineland wine, stone and ironware. Improvements were gradually made to the route which passed along the River Amstel and the River Vecht at Weesp, the Weesp Canal, the Rivers Gaasp and Smal to the Vaartse Rhine. It was known as the "Cologne Route". In 1825 it was extended when the new Zederik Canal was dug from Vianen to Gorcum. As a result of continued growth in traffic, another new section, the Merwede Canal from Zeeburg (Amsterdam) to the Vaartse Rhine (South of Utrecht), was opened in 1893. Even though the new canal was navigable for ships of up to 1200 tons, shipping was still restricted by low bridges and narrow locks. In 1931 the construction of an Amsterdam-Rhine Canal to connect into the River Waal at Tiel, and with a connection to the River Lek at Vreeswijk, was recommended. The new canal initially makes use of a widened and deepened Merwede Canal west of Utrecht, and then is new all the way to the River Waal. The completed canal was opened with celebrations on the 21st May 1952.

The Amsterdam-Rhine Canal connects the Dutch capital to its European hinterland.

The original Rotterdam harbour approach.

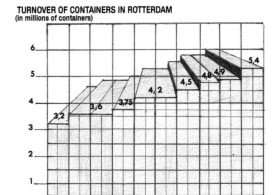

TURNOVER OF CONTAINERS IN ROTTERDAM
(in millions of containers)

Postcards showing Rotterdam services.

Rotterdam and the New Waterway

Many Dutch harbours situated on the North Sea coast are affected by silting. Measures such as laying down groynes and dredging the approach channels are taken to minimise the effects. Rotterdam's original approach to the sea was via the Voornsche Canal and the Brielsche Gat. This began to silt up around 1830. The second Thorbecke government passed legislation in 1863 for the creation of a direct connection to the North Sea. Pieter Caland (1826-1902) was in charge of the project, work commencing in 1866 and being completed in 1872.

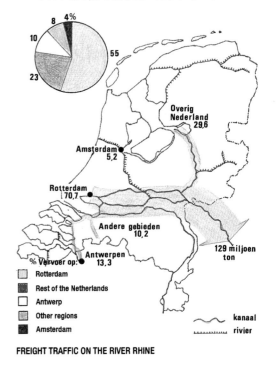

Overig
Nederland
29,6

Amsterdam
5,2

Rotterdam
70,7

Andere gebieden
10,2

Antwerpen
13,3

129 miljoen
ton

% Vervoer op:
- Rotterdam
- Rest of the Netherlands
- Antwerp
- Other regions
- Amsterdam

kanaal
river

FREIGHT TRAFFIC ON THE RIVER RHINE

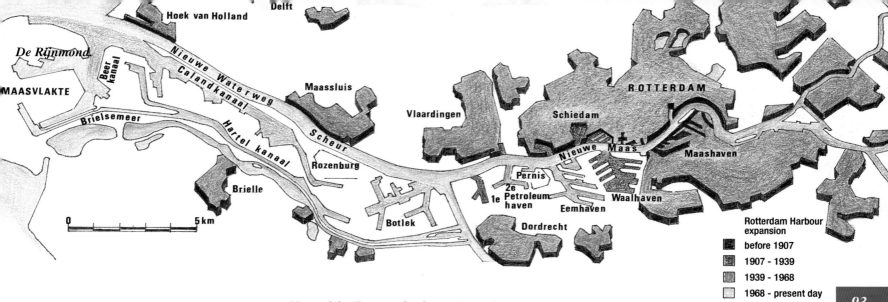

Hoek van Holland

Delft

De Rijnmond

MAASVLAKTE

Beer kanaal

Nieuwe Waterweg

Calandkanaal

Brielsemeer

Hartel kanaal

Scheur

Maassluis

Vlaardingen

ROTTERDAM

Schiedam

Nieuwe Maas

Maashaven

Rozenburg

Pernis

2e Petroleum haven

Eemhaven

Waalhaven

Brielle

Botlek

Dordrecht

0   5 km

Rotterdam Harbour
expansion

before 1907

1907 - 1939

1939 - 1968

1968 - present day

View of the Erasmus bridge at Rotterdam.

In contrast to the situation at Amsterdam, sea-going ships can sail directly into the harbour without having to pass through locks.
Due to its location at the mouth of a delta, Rotterdam has access to an extensive hinterland. The Ruhr valley for instance is only a part of this, and Rotterdam has made full use of its strategic position. Since the end of the Second World War Rotterdam has grown to become the largest transit harbour in Europe and it has the largest container terminal in the world.

Ferry services

From the point of view of road transport network, the waterways are an obstruction. At crossing points a ferry service can offer an interim solution when traffic volumes are not sufficient to justify construction of a bridge or tunnel. The ferry can also offer a safe open means of transport for dangerous loads.

Ferry traffic is a frequent phenomenon in the Netherlands. Flying ferries are to be found on the river crossings. The strong current makes it necessary to anchor the ferry at a midpoint in the river to prevent it being carried downstream. The cable is held above water by lighters . The ferry can then cross by a combination of motor power and current.

Westervoort flying ferry across the Nederrijn.

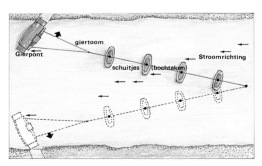

Diagram showing operation of a flying ferry.

94

The ferry across the North Sea Canal at Velsen.

Old postcard showing the Alkmaar Pakket.

Express ferry service

This chapter has outlined the historical significance of water transport. It is significant that the latest development is the utilisation of fast hydrofoils to provide commuter services over water. Attaining speeds of 70 km an hour they provide an alternative for the daily road traffic queues.

The ferries at canal crossings have no need of such a facility and operate with a normal ferryboat. In the provinces of North-Holland and Zeeland there are still ferries on strategically important routes. For instance at Den Helder the ferry crosses the Marsdiep to serve the island of Texel.

In Zeeland there are two ferry connections to Zeeuws- Vlaanderen, namely Vlissingen-Breskens and Kruiningen- Perkpolder. The first mentioned ferry connection is about to be replaced by a new tunnel currently under construction under the Westerschelde.

Tunnel connection

The increasing costs of the ferry make the construction of a tunnel economically viable. Map showing the route of the Scheldetunnel.

The hydrofoil operating between IJmuiden and Amsterdam as an alternative for train and bus.

Ferryboats on the service across the Westerschelde between Vlissingen and Breskens.

1

8 WATER AS A SOURCE OF FOOD

For centuries the Dutch fishing industry has played an important role. Today's techniques have become so intensive that quotas have to be applied to prevent over-fishing. In the near future more durable techniques will be necessary to achieve a balance.

2

3

The fishing industry

The Netherlands' maritime situation has provided generations of its fishermen with a living. In the past the life was hard. The familiar cutters and luggers drifted for weeks on the open sea. The crew's diet consisted of rice, rancid bacon and beer. Drinking water was scarce. In spite of this hard life, the fishers' tales always reflected their attachment to the trade. The wooden flat-bottoms were pulled up onto the beach to load and unload and were pulled back into the sea by teams of horses. In the town the fish was smoked and packed into barrels. In the winter the fishermen repaired the sails and rigging and mended the nets. Their wives brought the catch to market.

1. At the beginning of the 20th century it was still possible to meet a fish seller.
2. In the winter there was time to repair the nets.
3. The whole family, both young and old, worked to keep the business going.
4. Flat-bottoms on the beach at Scheveningen (Panorama Mesdag).

The fishermen wore woollen clothing, a cap, a flap-dungaree and short jacket, and a golden earring. The ring was not only for identification purposes but was also a life insurance. When his body was retrieved, a drowned fisherman could be identified and his funeral could be paid for by the ring. Because of the nature of his work it would have been dangerous to wear a ring on his finger, so the earring was also his wedding ring.

Organisation of the fishing business

The Netherlands has always made a distinction between small and large-scale fishing. Deep-sea drift net fishing for herring has traditionally been classed as the large-scale activity, as was long- line fishing and trawling for cod and haddock at the end of the nineteenth century.

Fishing in the Zuiderzee and the Waddenzee, and along the North sea coast and in the sea-arms, is classed as small-scale activity. The mussel- and oyster bed culture in Zeeland also belong to this sector of the industry even though they are internationally famous.

The fishing harbour at Scheveningen makes a colourful sight in the spring when the first basket of herring is landed and auctioned. The fishing boats along the quayside are bedecked in flags.

Long-line fishing for mackerel in 1880.

A jolly advertising poster.

Drift net fishing

In the past Holland was internationally famous for this form of fishing. The equipment consisted of a number of nets, each 30 metres long and 16 metres deep. The drift net could be up to 4 km long and was suspended with weights to keep it taught like a curtain hanging in the sea. Floats or buoys were attached at regular intervals and kept together by a float line on which the drift net was hung by seizings.

Drift net fishing-
the net is drawn aboard.

The fishing boats were originally timber built, and later steel-hulled. The hull shape depended on the fishing technique to be adopted. At the end of the 19th century the sailboat had to make way for steam. The steam era lasted till around 1960. The modern fishing fleet consists of cutters and trawlers.

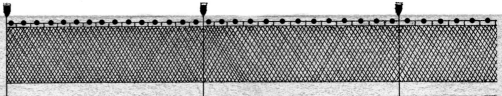

Trawling the bobbin line is being cast free.

Herring barrels- quayside at Vlaardingen.

A steam trawler on the open sea.

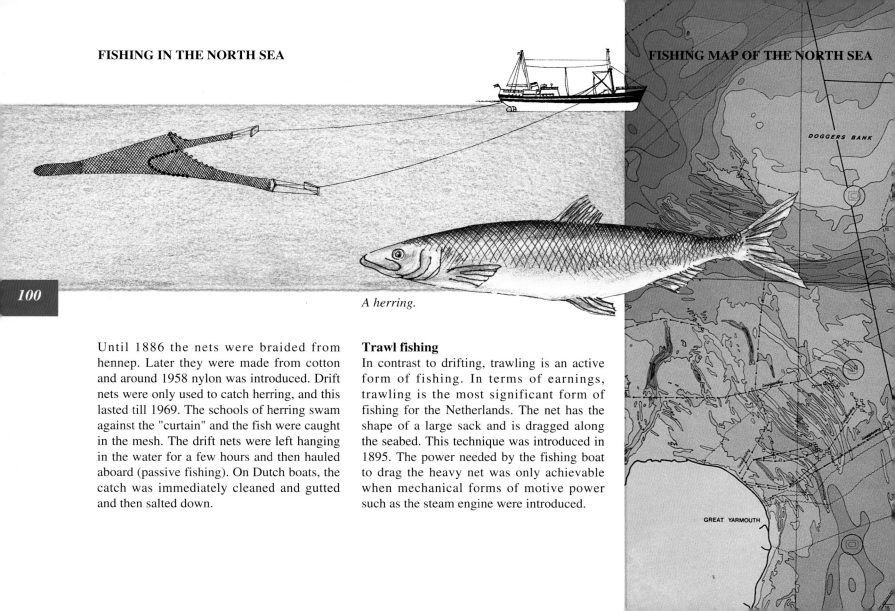

A herring.

DOGGERS BANK

GREAT YARMOUTH

Until 1886 the nets were braided from hennep. Later they were made from cotton and around 1958 nylon was introduced. Drift nets were only used to catch herring, and this lasted till 1969. The schools of herring swam against the "curtain" and the fish were caught in the mesh. The drift nets were left hanging in the water for a few hours and then hauled aboard (passive fishing). On Dutch boats, the catch was immediately cleaned and gutted and then salted down.

Trawl fishing
In contrast to drifting, trawling is an active form of fishing. In terms of earnings, trawling is the most significant form of fishing for the Netherlands. The net has the shape of a large sack and is dragged along the seabed. This technique was introduced in 1895. The power needed by the fishing boat to drag the heavy net was only achievable when mechanical forms of motive power such as the steam engine were introduced.

100

Boom fishing.

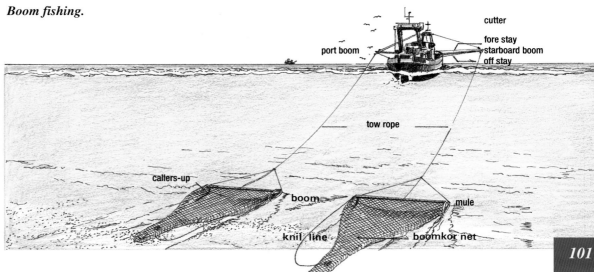

The mouth of the trawl net is kept open by floats on the top side, and by heavy belly ropes which keep the bottom open. Trawl boards attached by tow ropes to the sides pull the opening apart. The trawl boards are angled in such a way that as the ship steams ahead the current forces the boards apart and opens the trawl net. The advantage of this technique is that the same ship and net can be used to catch several sorts of fish, including herring.

The disadvantage is that the trawl is not selective and drags the seabed clean, taking small fish and leading to over-fishing.

Boom fishing
This technique has taken prime place in the Dutch fishing industry. The method dates from the 16th century or even earlier. The scrub or boom net is dragged along the seabed by small vessels. The net is kept open at the sides by a wooden boom.

Diagram of a boom net

Labels on diagram: Buik, Kuil, Korboom of boom, Sprenkels van de korlijn, Slof

About 40 x a year

Diagram of a boom net

Braces are fixed at the extremities of the boom which slide on the seabed and prevent damage to the net. Chains are attached to the underside of the net to make fish jump up into it. The arrival of the steam trawler at end of last century signalled the end of scrub net fishing. After the Second World War the coastal fishing industry needed a method for catching the seabed fish. The trawl net was not the answer and older techniques were revived. Modern cutters fish with two boom nets lowered into the sea on either side of the vessel.

TABLE OF TASKS ON BOARD A FISHING VESSEL

Departure
↓
Casting nets
↓
Fishing
↓
Hauling nets
↓
Processing
↓
Packing
↓
Return to port

The most cutters perform tightly scheduled voyages of a week's duration.
Departure Monday morning early to the fishing grounds and casting the nets. Two to three hours fishing.
Processing the first catch. Thursday end of fishing and return to port in time for Friday fish auction.
Weekend fitting out the ship for next voyage.

A fishing cutter in Scheveningen harbour.

Design of a modern cutter 2000

The skipper is alone on an increasingly technically equipped bridge. He is kept informed by radio of weather conditions and catches made by colleagues. He keeps records in the logbook. He also functions as lookout. He is relieved for rest periods by a crew-member.

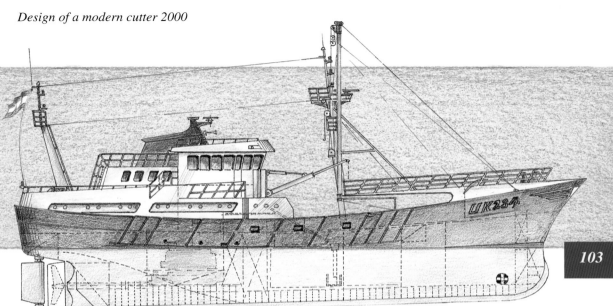

The cutter

There are actually three types of ship combined in this modern fishing vessel. The tugboat is needed to tow the fishing tackle, the factory ship to process the catch and the refrigerated vessel to transport the catch back and unload it at the harbour. The modern cutter has an overall length of 20 to 40 metres, and is equipped with a marine engine of 300 to 2000 horsepower. The cruising speed of these vessels is around 16 to 26 km an hour. They usually carry a crew of six. The modern cutter is equipped with the latest navigational aids, such as satellite navigation, an electronic chart and radar, in order to fix a position any time of night or day. The radar helps to avoid collisions with other ships. It will not be long before equipment becomes available for locating the particular type of fish to be caught.

Sensing equipment

The bridge is equipped with special instruments for sensing the fish (see previous page).

The echoing sound waves are recorded on a roll of paper to produce an "echogram". In this way schools of fish can be located. Experienced skippers can even recognise fish types from the echogram plot (see illustration below).

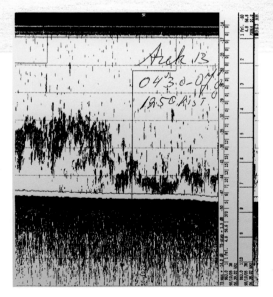

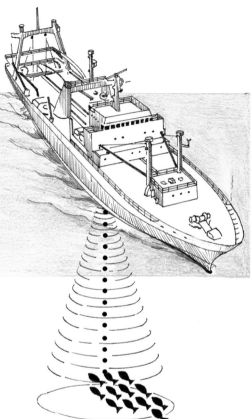

The echolode consists of a transmitter producing sound waves. These travel through the water at a speed of 1500 metres per second.

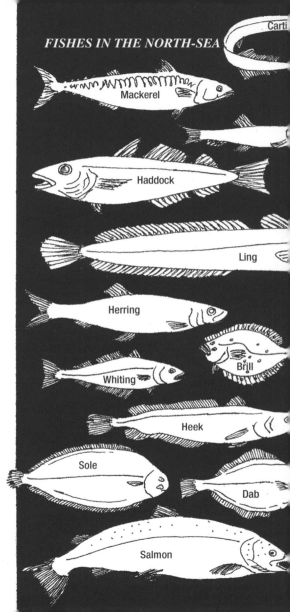

FISHES IN THE NORTH-SEA

Carti

Mackerel

Haddock

Ling

Herring

Brill

Whiting

Heek

Sole

Dab

Salmon

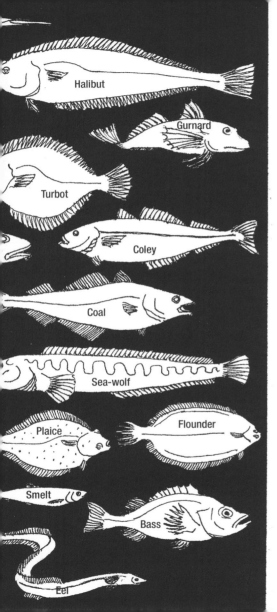

Halibut

Gurnard

Turbot

Coley

Coal

Sea-wolf

Plaice

Flounder

Smelt

Bass

Eel

Special fishing nets
These days use is also made of a floating
(Pelagic) net, which can be steered by means
of sonar.

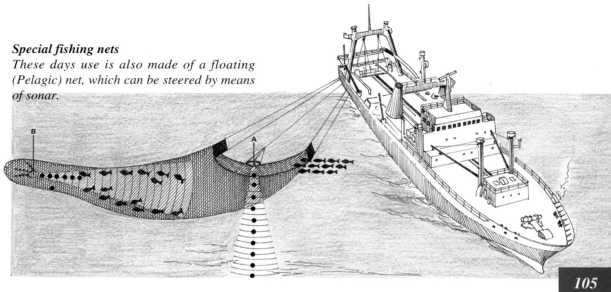

Consumption and export

In contrast to the enormous quantities of fish always landed, the level of domestic consumption has never been very great. Fish used to be regarded as a second-rate food good for common folk, although it is in fact highly nourishing.

As a result, the Dutch fishing industry has always targeted the export market. In 1900 this extended to countries as such as Germany, Russia and America. In order to guarantee exports the whole year round,

Dutch fishermen had to look for fishing grounds further from home. This necessitated even larger ships and these became too expensive to finance for a modest fisherman. Large companies were set up to lease the ships. The fishermen from the island of Urk, who fished in the Zuiderzee prior to the construction of the enclosing dike, have built up a reputation for long distance fishing, even reaching the shores of Africa on their long voyages.

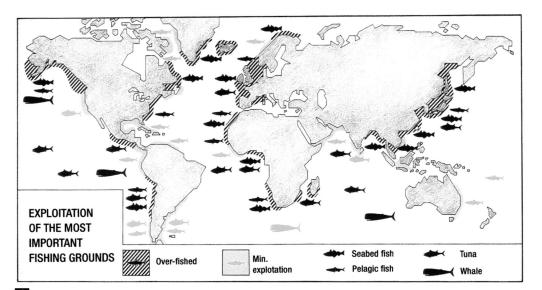

EXPLOITATION OF THE MOST IMPORTANT FISHING GROUNDS

▨ Over-fished ▨ Min. exploitation ◄►◄ Seabed fish ◄►◄ Pelagic fish ◄►◄ Tuna ◤ Whale

1

STATISTICS OF DUTCH FISHING INDUSTRY

Quota in tons	1985	1986	1987	1988
Sole	16515	14270	10985	10310
Plaice	81620	79500	64670	78970
Cod	28720	17670	14700	17550
Herring	80696	95790	99100	88450
Mackerel	35330	32370	36210	36410
Whiting	9670	12592	7900	6770
Coley	210	260	210	200
Haddock	2070	1630	1040	1330
Sea-devil		210	315	690
Sprat	1950	30000	50000	50000
Heek	90	120	110	310
Hors Mackerel	175000	112250	147250	160750
Blue Whiting	277000	315000	308500	308500
Kever	340000	300000	171000	200000

2

Current catch limitations

The tendency to build larger and more powerful ships has not lost its momentum, and the vessels can almost be described as floating factories. This scaling-up has taken place since the Second World War. The costs have spiralled and this necessitates even larger catches in order to be able to finance the large vessels and keep them in operation. The resulting over-fishing presents a problem for the whole of the Dutch fishing industry.

Besides, Holland is not the only fishing nation. The Netherlands' membership of the European Union and the growing awareness in Europe that there is a danger of wiping out fish stocks altogether, has led to the setting up of safeguarding arrangements. The amount of fish per sort is determined every year in the form of a "quota". It is clear that this has caused problems for many fishermen who have seen their incomes falling as a result.

This is made worse by the fact that interest rates have also been increasing. The solution to these problems will have to be found in a restructuring of the industry.

1. A review of the world's major fishing grounds.
2. The table gives the fish quota's laid down to prevent over-fishing.

CROSS SECTION OF A MODERN TRAWLER

1. Cockpit
2. Bridge
3. Cabins
4. Engine room

5. Fish deck
6. Fish handling area
7. Fish winch
8. Freezers and working deck

9. Deep frozen hold
10. Steering propeller
11. Lifeboat
12. Propeller & Rudder

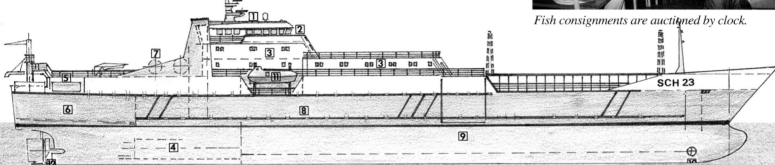

Fish consignments are auctioned by clock.

The fish auction

Early in the morning the crates of fish are unloaded from the ships and collected in a spacious hall. The same catches and the fish sort are stacked together. The fish has already been sorted by size on the ship. The buyers judge quality, quantity and decide a price. Fish destined for abroad is loaded into freezer lorries.

The fish auction in IJmuiden.

The former island of Schokland at high tide.

Old fishing ports

The towns around the Zuiderzee such as Hoorn, Enkhuizen, Volendam, and others such as Spakenburg, Hardewijk and Elburg, have always been fishing ports. The island dwellers of Marken, Urk and Schokland were fisher folk making a living from fishing in the Zuiderzee.

The closing off of the Zuiderzee from the sea in 1932 was for many fishermen fatal. They were forced to choose another livelihood. On the North Sea coast, Den Helder, Zandvoort, Noordwijk, Katwijk and Scheveningen were important fishing towns. On the South-Holland islands lying in the river mouths of the delta there were countless small fishing communities. On the South-Holland island of Goeree-Overflakee fishing is the tradition. Goedereede and Middelharnis were well-known fishing ports. In this area the fishing was generally combined with trading. Fish was exchanged for wine. On the one hand the

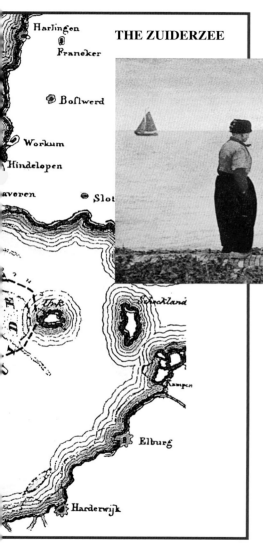

THE ZUIDERZEE

Taking leave of the Zuiderzee fishery.

The outdoor museum at Enkhuizen.

trade was a source of employment for the region and it generated new income, and on the other hand it required the provision of new facilities. The local authority created new harbour facilities such as quaysides, storage sheds, markets and beacons.

The Zuiderzee fishing industry

Closure of the Zuiderzee in 1932 signalled the end of an era for the fishermen here. When the dike was completed there were large numbers of anchovy, shrimp, smelt, flounder, blei & sprot, eel and herring enclosed in the new lake. The fisher folk expected to see a layer of dead fish on the surface but this never materialised. The variety of fish sorts has gradually reduced since the closure. Before the war the Nederlandse Heidemaatschappij had sown a large number of fry, but only the eel and the pike-perch have survived in the new environment. The eel evolved from the saltwater variety with its thin skin into the

The fishing village of Volendam has retained much of its original character.

IJsselmeer fishermen are a dying race.

popular freshwater sort with a thicker skin. The smoking of the eel provides a little employment and the fish stalls do good business to the tourists who visit places such as Urk and Volendam. Thanks to the eel, a remnant of the fishing industry has survived on the IJsselmeer to provide employment to a number of fishermen. The fishing port of Urk has retained its importance. The Urker fishermen are willing to sail far from their home base.

Urk is the largest centre in Europe for trading in plaice and sole. The most IJsselmeer fishers still sailing have no successor. The younger generation see no future in the fishing industry. During the season the IJsselmeer has become the domain of pleasure boats.

Fisheries in the delta

A similar process has taken place on the estuaries of the river delta as that on the Zuider-zee. Following the flood disaster of 1953, the government decided to close off the sea arms of the delta, to prevent incursion by the sea in times of storm. The region was a rich harvest ground for a variety of fish and this was a heavy blow for the industry. However the modern technique can adjust to environmental demands, and as a result of strong protests from the environmental lobby and other interested parties, the plan was amended to close the Oosterschelde by means

Old fishing smacks lie along the quayside in the harbour at Vlaardingen.

The mobile fish stall offering all kinds of tasty morsels is a common sight at the seaside resorts in Holland. The traditional pickled and salted herring are very popular with the seaside visitors.

of a pile dam. In this way the oyster and mussel culture of the area which is dependent on the effects of tide could be retained. Nevertheless several kinds of migratory fish have disappeared from the region, because they could no longer reach the spawning grounds as a result of the placing of the new dams. In addition, the shipping channels were dredged in order to deepen them, resulting in the destruction of the underwater environment.

Open fishing fleet day in the Scheveningen harbour.

There was already an element of over-fishing due to more efficient fishing techniques, and this was accompanied by pollution due to dumping of effluents. Currently sluices in the dams along the coast are opened at low tide to reactivate currents of freshwater with the result that salmon and sea trout have to an extent returned. The Dutch lakes and canals are among the richest in fish life, because it is easier to achieve water quality control, and new fish can be seeded.

WATER AS ALLY

On the beach the children build their sandcastles.
It must be in our genes. This natural defensive urge has evolved
down the centuries to culminate in the strategic defensive flood lines
so characteristic of the Netherlands.

112

Castle and moat

In the early Middle Ages, the aristocracy built their castles at strategic points in order to confirm and maintain their feudal power. The term castle is derived from the Latin word "castellum". The earliest type was the "moat" castle. The castle was built on an artificial mound or "motte". The wooden keep (living space) was surrounded by a palisade and the motte was surrounded by a ditch filled with water (moat). Access to the castle was via a bridge.

A reconstruction of the ring castle at Oostvoorne (from a drawing by A.L.Oger).

The oldest fortification was surrounded by a wooden palisade and a "dry ditch".

KEY

1. Mound (Motte)	**9.** Arcade
2. Stone bridge	**10.** Merlon
3. Drawbridge	**11.** Window
4. Outer bailey	**12.** Keep
5. Gate tower	**13.** Stair
6. Lookout towers	**14.** Open tower
7. Cage	**15.** Closed tower
8. Battlements	**16.** Platform

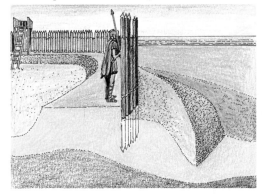

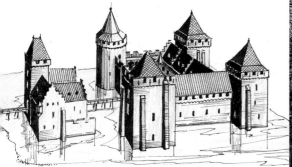

Schematic reconstruction drawing of ruins Brederode "complete".

From 1100 the wooden palisade was replaced by one made of brick. The establishment of such a fortification was a sovereign right. The sovereign entrusted this right to feudal lords, who were then responsible for the government in their area.

The ruin of Brederode castle at Santpoort is an early example of a water castle. During the eighty years war the Spanish captured the castle and it has never been restored.

The Muiderslot gives a good impression of life in a Medieval castle.

The lord lived with his family and servants in the castle. The size of the building reflected his wealth. In Holland the oldest fortifications have a round form and are provided with a water moat. In the second half of the 13t century, the influence of Floris V resulted in a change in castle design to a square floor plan with a tower at each corner.

It was easier to defend the walls from the projecting towers and the attackers could be struck in the flank. The invention of gunpowder and the introduction of the cannon rendered the castle vulnerable. The stone walls could no longer withstand a sustained bombardment. The castle was replaced in the military sense by the fort and in the domestic sense by the mansion. Fortunately there are a number of reasonable examples of castles and romantic ruins in Holland.

The Morschpoort at Leiden.

The growth of towns

In the later Middle Ages a third class of citizen, the commoner, appeared on the scene. The development of the town surrounded by a pro-tective wall, allowed the citizens to exercise their crafts in relative peace. Once a city had received a charter from the ruling lord, it was allowed to build walls and gates. The residents within were from then on called "citizens". The city was ruled by a

A timber frame was built as basis for the first town houses. The walls were made of reeds and loam. The brick wall and tiles ap-peared later. In the Lowlands piles had to be driven in the ground to give a firm founda-tion for the houses (1).

The " moat castle" at Leiden (2 & 3) stands on a mound at the confluence of two arms of the river Rhine. At its foot the first settlement grew up.

Hoorn is a picturesque port at the Ysselmeer.

The Keizersgracht in Amsterdam.

The Kenaupark in Haarlem.

mayor supported by his sheriffs. The militia provided security. At sunset the gates were closed and the drawbridges pulled up. Encircled by a wide moat the citizens could neither come in or go out. As in modern times, so in those days too, the maintenance of an army was a costly business. The costs of maintaining the city defences weighed on its citizenry, and was particularly onerous in times of economic decline. However it was essential for a busy town with an increasing population to expand on the periphery. A good example of such expansion are the seventeenth century concentric canals surrounding the historical centre of Amsterdam. They show up clearly as strong structural elements on the city plan. Many Dutch towns expanded in this way, although not so spectacularly as the city of Amsterdam. In the second half of the 19th century most towns demolished their city walls.

As a result of the explosive economic growth experienced at this time, space was created for the increasing traffic. In a number of Dutch towns, the bastions were landscaped and became pleasant city parks.

Historical city gate at Amersfoort.

The Eighty Years War 1568-1648

Stadhouder Maurits (1567-1625).

This war was of great significance into the existence history of The Netherlands. At this time, Spain was part of the Habsburg empire. The German emperor, Charles V, was king of Spain and ruler of the Netherlands. Charles V abdicated in 1555.

The war began as a rebellion against the Spanish domination and the central power at Brussel when Philip II, son of Charles V, departed to Spain.

Philip II, developed a strategy whereby Spain played an increasingly crucial role. The Habsburgers saw themselves as the protectors of the Catholic Church.

In the Lowlands, the Reformation fell on fertile soil. Philip II, supported by the Duke of Alva, despatched a powerful army to the North to restore order. His bloody attempts to stamp out heresy had an adverse effect. Many Dutch towns such as Haarlem, Alkmaar and Leiden chose the side of William of Orange. Williams sons, Maurits and Frederik Hendrik, proved to be able military leaders. Thanks to them, the rebellious republic achieved ascendancy in the continuing struggle.

On 30th January 1648, the peace of Munster was signed, establishing the independence of the republic.

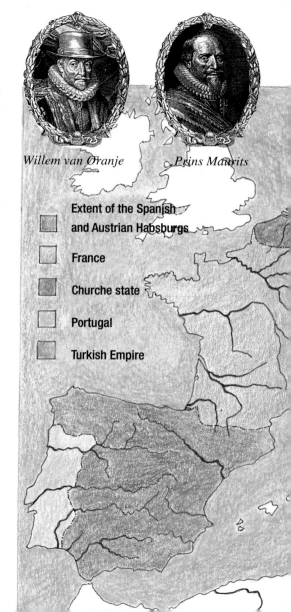

Willem van Oranje   *Prins Maurits*

Extent of the Spanish and Austrian Habsburgs

France

Churche state

Portugal

Turkish Empire

116

Phillips II

Hertog Alva

On 1st April 1572, the Watergeuzen led by Admiral Lumey marched to Den Briel, a town strategically situated at the mouth of the Meuse. It was the first town to be taken by the rebels. The verse "In the name of Orange, open the city gates, the Watergeuzen have reached den Briel" immortalises this event. The town became a stronghold of the rebellion against Spain.

A musketeer.

Spanish conquerors on a headstone in Naarden.

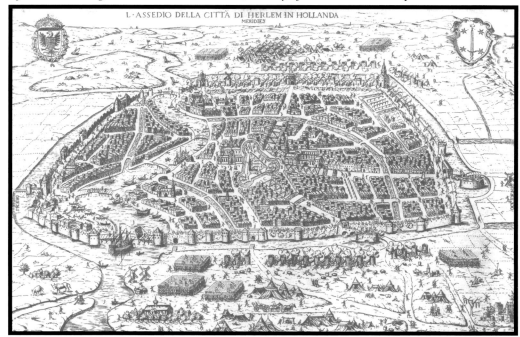

L·ASSEDIO DELLA CITTÀ DI HERLEM IN HOLLANDA
MERIDIES

THE VICTORY BEGINS AT ALKMAAR (21-08 to 08-10 in 1573)

In the 15th and 16th centuries the towns were protected by walls and moats and this presented an obstacle for the enemy and a valuable asset until well into the eighty years war. In the long run, the brick walls, bastions and city gates were not a match for sustained attacks. The sieges involving barrages by cannon eventually breached the city walls, allowing the enemy infantry to infiltrate the town. For both sides the siege was a war of attrition. Nevertheless important towns such as Haarlem, Alkmaar and Leiden chose to offer resistance because they feared the lot of Zutphen and Naarden whose populations were totally wiped out.

After an enduring and heroic battle in 1573, the city of Haarlem had to capitulate.

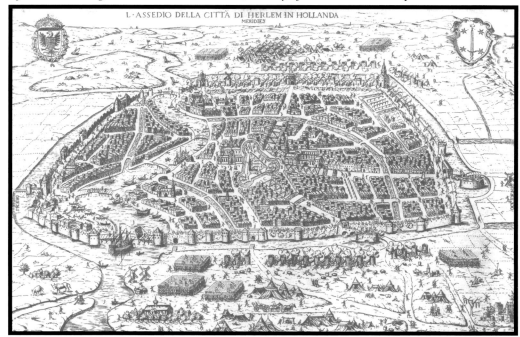

118

TOT EER VAN HAER GESLAGT TOT LOF VAN DESE DAAD
DIE KLAMPEN HEM AEN BOORT DIE WETEN NOCH WEL RAEDT
HIER IS EEN HOORNS HOP, DAER GAET 'T OP EEN VEGHTEN

DAER SIET MEN 'T EENE SCHIP VAST AEN 'T ANDER HEGHTEN
DAER SIET MEN REGHTE LIEFDE DAER DOET MEN ONDERSTANT
DAER VEGHT MEN SONDER GELT VOOR 'T LIEVE VADERLAND

On the 11th of October 1573, the Watergeuzen defeated the Spanish on the Zuiderzee (from a house in Hoorn).

A map of the siege of Alkmaar (1573).

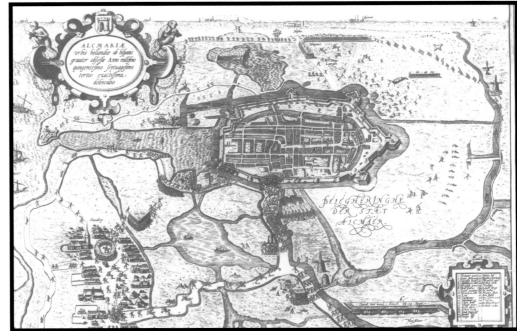

After defeating Haarlem the Spanish forces marched to Alkmaar. They were held off and the victory for the republic dawned.

MENNO VAN COEHOORN (1641-1704)

The fortified town of Coevorden.

Baron Menno van Coehoorn was the chief strategist of the Republic of the United Netherlands during the rule of stadhouder Willem III. He displayed great professionalism in publishing a defence plan for Coevorden. His publication "New fortification on a wet or low horizon" brought him fame on a European level.

Fortified towns

As has become apparent from the previous description, the power and range of artillery has largely determined the development of fortified towns. A characteristic Dutch form of fortification developed during the eighty years war, which lasted with short pauses from 1568 till the peace of Munster was signed in 1648. At the start of the rebellion against Spanish rule, the towns were still

Many South- and North-Holland forti-fications were improved or renewed by Menno van Coehorn. The defences of Bergen op Zoom are considered to be his masterpiece (demolished in 1869). The As-sociation for the Preservation of Historic Fortifications bears his name.

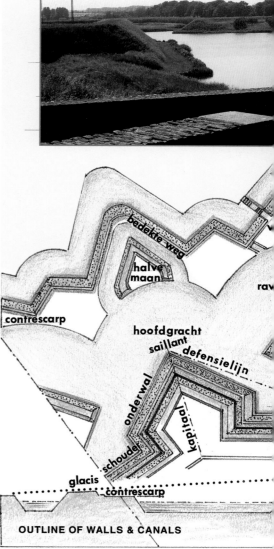

Cross-section and plan of a historical Dutch

KEY

1. *Vriesse Gate*
2. *Ravelijn*
3. *Powder house*
4. *Bastion*
5. *Standerd Mill*
6. *Contrescarp*
7. *Munterse Gate*

The earthen banks around Heusden.

The fortified town of Bourtange is located on a sandy mound in marshland. It was the only access point on the eastern side of Groninger country.

surrounded by Medieval walls and towers. Since neither time or money was available for expensive and complicated works, SimonStevin was responsible for developing a simple system of earthen dikes which was copied by many towns. In the seventeenth century this system was improved by Menno van Coehoorn. His system was known as the "New Netherlands" fortification system. He surrounded the town in question with bastions of a geometric pattern tailor-made for the situation. His genius lay in his ability to make use of the local hydraulic characteristics of the land.

121

Loevestein Castle is located at the confluence of the rivers Meuse and Rhine. Earthen embankments were later thrown up around it to resist attack by gunfire.

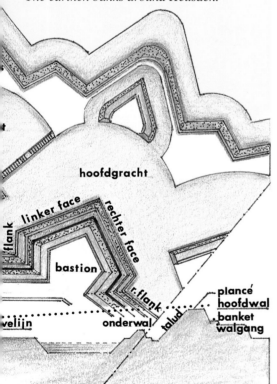

bastion (from a sketch by N.H.Schukkings)

The Dutch water defence line

The water defence line represents an unusually interesting method of protecting a country from invasion by the enemy. It is almost impossible to mount a battle on flooded land. In times of hostilities, the land surrounding the towns was inundated to keep the artillery out of range.

In 1672, the water line was used successfully against the French troops of King Louis XIV. After 1874 it was officially known as the "New Holland Water Defence Line".

In the course of history, the line has moved gradually eastwards to a point beyond U-trecht. The Defence Department had installed sluices at many points to be better able to control the whole area.

The town hall at Nieuwpoort on the Lek is strategically placed above a sluice gate.

This map shows the extent of the Holland water defence line. It was an important way of protecting the country by means of inundation.

The star-shaped fortification of Naarden forms part of the Holland water defence line.

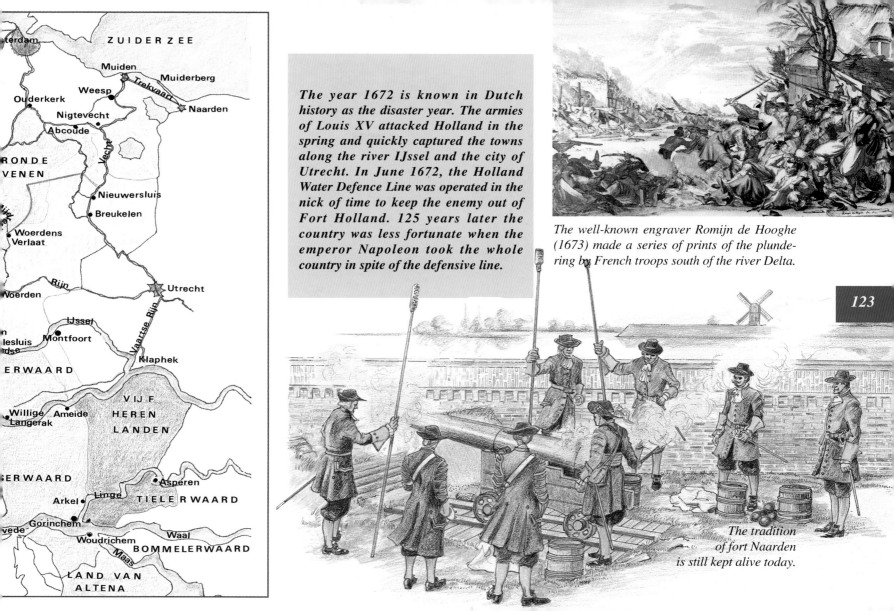

The year 1672 is known in Dutch history as the disaster year. The armies of Louis XV attacked Holland in the spring and quickly captured the towns along the river IJssel and the city of Utrecht. In June 1672, the Holland Water Defence Line was operated in the nick of time to keep the enemy out of Fort Holland. 125 years later the country was less fortunate when the emperor Napoleon took the whole country in spite of the defensive line.

The well-known engraver Romijn de Hooghe (1673) made a series of prints of the plundering by French troops south of the river Delta.

123

The tradition of fort Naarden is still kept alive today.

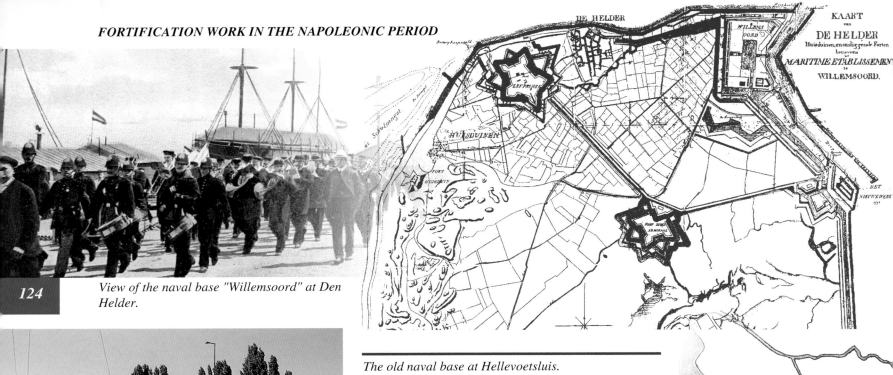

KAART
van
DE HELDER
Huisduinen, en omliggende Forten
benevens
MARITIME ETABLISSEMENT
te
WILLEMSOORD.

124

View of the naval base "Willemsoord" at Den Helder.

The old naval base at Hellevoetsluis.

Forts and bunkers

Due to the increase in range and devastation of grenades, the construction of forts needed to be more effective. The first measure to be implemented was the removal of the upper levels to reduce the profile of the fort. In the nineteenth century the distance around the towns had to be increased to form a

The New Holland Water Defence Line.

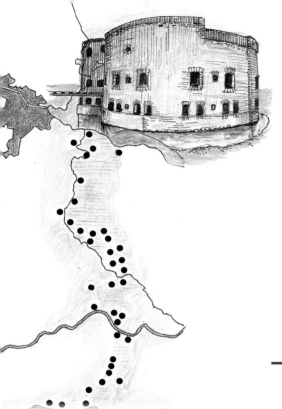

The fort at Muiden was intended to protect the sea locks situated at the mouth of the river Vecht and which formed part of the Holland Water Defence Line. It goes without saying that the farmers in the area were less enthusiastic about the prospect of having their fields inundated. Finally, a compensation scheme was drawn up.

In 1815, King Willem I gave orders to expand the Holland Water Defence Line to include the city of Utrecht. The schematic map shows clearly how the city is shielded by a ring of forts and so brought within the defensive system.

To give extra protection to the Water Defence Line flat-bottomed patrol boats equipped with canon were brought into service.

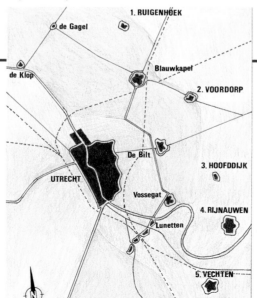

sufficiently safe barrier. Initially brick was used as building material, protected by a layer of earth. Later reinforced concrete and armoured steel plate was introduced. The forts were camouflaged with shrubbery and slopes landscaped with trees.
The Defence Department had installed sluices

at many points to be better able to control the water system of the whole area. In de course of history, the line has moved gradually eastwards to keep cities as Utrecht outside the reach of the modern artillerie. After 1922, the New Holland Water Defence Line was in fact the Eastern Front of " Fort Holland."

The Amsterdam Defence Line

KEY

1. Muiden	19. Spaarndam-Noord
2. Weesp	20. Zuidwijkermeer
3. Nigtevecht	21. Velsen
4. Abcoude	22. St.Aagtendijk
5. Winkel	23. Veldhuis
6. Botshol	24. Ham
7. Waversamstel	25. Krommeniedijk
8. Uithoorn	26. Marken-Binnen
9. Drecht	27. Spijkerboor
10. Kwakel	28. Jisperweg
11. Kudelstaart	29. Middenweg
12. Aalsmeer	30. Nekkerweg
13. Hoofddorp	31. Purmerend
14. Vijfhuizen	32. Kwadijk
15. Liede	33. Edam
16. Liebrug	34. Durgerdam
17. Penningsveer	35. Pampus
18. Spaarndam-Zuid	36. Diemerdam

Forts also part of the Holland Water Defence Line.
1. Naarden 2. Uitermeer 3. Hinderdam
4. Kijkuit 5. Spion 6. Nieuwersluis 7. Tienhoven

— Sections of wall
--- Old section of water defence line from 1887 and 1889
// // // // Hatched lines show northern Section of water defence line

The line is 135 km in length and was meant to act as a back up should the troops retreat from the Holland Water Defence Line. In 1951, after the Second World War, the status of the line was rescinded by Royal Consent.

The fort at Spaarndam.

Fort Pampus.

The more than forty forts installed in a circle around the city is known as the "stelling" or defence line of Amsterdam. The line was a result of the new 'Defence Act' of 1874.

Amsterdam Defence Line, Utrecht 1910 (information W.E.van Dam van Isselt).

The fort at Spijkerboor. The gun turret houses two 10,5 cm. rapid fire cannon.

Since 1996 the line has been placed on the World Heritage List drawn up by UNESCO. The circle of forts is military very impressive and unique. In fact is the circle a Dutch translation of the French " Maginot Line." Nowadays is the circle also ecologically interesting, because it represents a natural habitat within an urbanised area. To encourage tourits to visit by bicycle the locations are included in a recreational cycle route.

Cross section of a revolving gun turret.

127

The forts offer protection against artillery.

Underground tunnel system inside the fort.

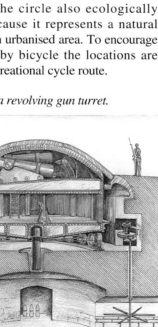

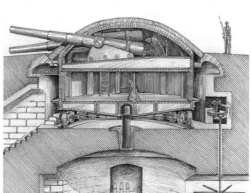

Defence lines in the Netherlands in 1940

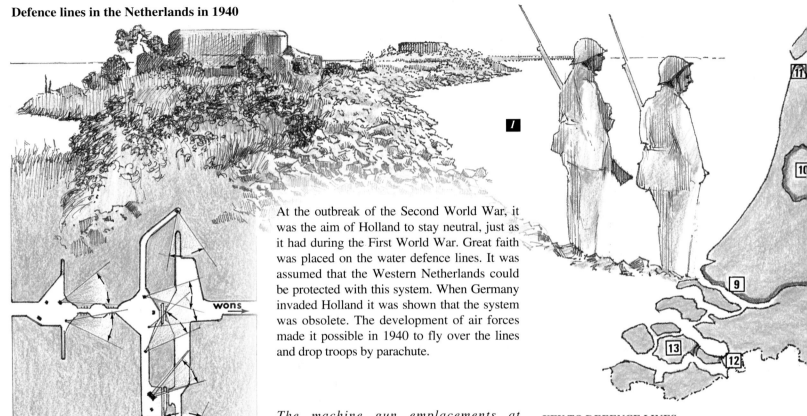

At the outbreak of the Second World War, it was the aim of Holland to stay neutral, just as it had during the First World War. Great faith was placed on the water defence lines. It was assumed that the Western Netherlands could be protected with this system. When Germany invaded Holland it was shown that the system was obsolete. The development of air forces made it possible in 1940 to fly over the lines and drop troops by parachute.

The machine gun emplacements at Kornwerderzand covered one another and the whole length of the enclosing dike. They proved to be impregnable and were only lost after the capitulation (1,2).

KEY TO DEFENCE LINES
1. Wons-position at Kornwerderzand. 2. IJssel - Maas position 3. Grebbel line 4. Betuwe position 5. Meuse-Waal position 6. Peel-Raam position 7. Waal-Linge position 8. New Holland Water

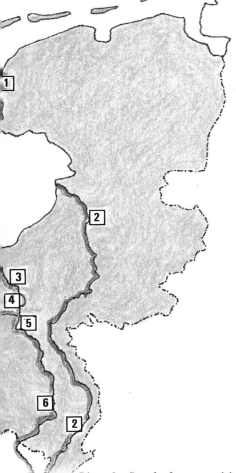

Dutch mounted troops equipped with cannon riding through inundated land (8 dec.1939).

At the Grebbeberg in the Gelder valley and at Kornwerderzand on the enclosing dike, it was possible to hold back the enemy attack. Especially the batteries in the modern bunkers at Kornwerderzand proved their effectiveness. Only when the enemy bombed Rotterdam and threatened to do the same to other cities, was the Netherlands forced to capitulate. A hostile modern air force had referred the defence lines to the scrap heap of history.

During the First World War many shelters were made of concrete. In the thirties hundreds of turrets for machine guns and cannon were constructed of this material.

Defence Line 9. South front position 10. Amsterdam Defence Line 11. Den Helder position 12. Bath position 13. Zanddijk position

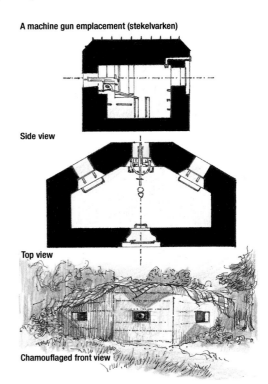

A machine gun emplacement (stekelvarken)

Side view

Top view

Chamouflaged front view

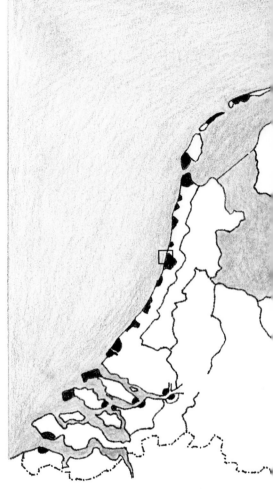

The map shows clearly how the whole of the coastline was defended against a possible invasion from the sea.

The Atlantic Wall

Plan of an artillery bunker

12,50 m

13,50 m

3

2   2

The design of the staircase was such as to prevent shells from ricochetting into the bunker.
1. Entrance; 2. Ammunition storage; 3. Gun mounting. The fire command post (below) was fitted with a range finder (4) The staff room, with telephone and radio communication (5) was situated on the floor below.

130 **Coastalbattery
in IJmuiden**

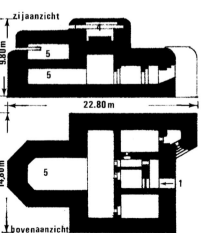

zijaanzicht

9,80 m

5

5

22.80 m

14,80 m

5

1

bovenaanzicht

The last item of this chapter is a relic of the German occupation. Many of the bunkers in the sea dunes still bear manifest evidence of this final defence line. In the war years ca.1500 bunkers for personnel, ammunition stores or machine gun and anti-aircraft turrets were built in the Netherlands.

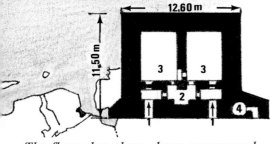

The floor plan above shows a personnel bunker, and the one under a machine gun emplacement.

Key:
1. Bunker entrance
2. Gas channel
3. Personnel
4. Lookout position
5. Machine gun
6. Close defence

The army had 120 standard bunker designs. The German marines had an extensive coastal battery available consisting of various designs. There were two standard designs for bunkers:

Type A: Walls and roof 3,5 metres thick reinforced concrete for protecting very important strategic objects such as the submarine harbour in IJmuiden.

Type B: Walls and roof 2 metres thick for normal strategic defensive works. Weathered by time they are now protected listed buildings.

A fragment of a tank wall in the dunes.

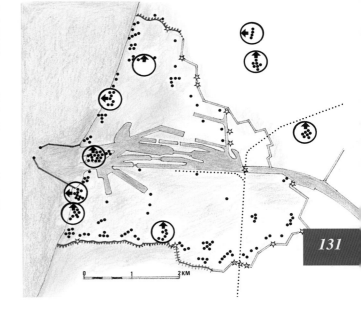

Key - "Festung IJmuiden" with standard defensive installations.

Coastal battery
Anti-aircraft battery
Tank ditch
Road block
Artificial dunes
Bunker
Tank wall
Hemm curves
Railway line

10 | WATER RECREATION

It is significant that water-based recreation, both in its active and passive forms, has become increasingly popular. It provides rest and relaxation in contrast to the busy pace of modern life.

Reinwardtstraat

19th century neighbourhood in Amsterdam.

Leisure time

The industrialisation in Europe in the second half of the nineteenth century laid the basis for a fundamental change in working patterns. Throughout the twentieth century the pro-portion of leisure time has steadily increased. Especially since the fifties, the growth in leisure activities has snowballed. First the Saturday was dropped as a working day in most industries and then the 40-hour

The illustrations right and left symbolise the contrast between life at the end of the 19th and at the end of the 20th century. High-rise living for a rapidly expanding urban population. The first timid bathers shown on the postcard were later to make way for mass tourism.

ZANDVOORT
In het bad

Frans van Seters.

week was introduced. This is still being successively amended and the number of holidays is growing. Early retirement and unem-ployment create a widening gap between work and leisure. Home life has also seen changes in this period. All kinds of domestic appliances have been introduced to make home chores easier. New houses required by a growing population mean the creation of new suburbs on the edge of towns. No wonder that urban flat dwellers swell the leisure crowds in good weather.

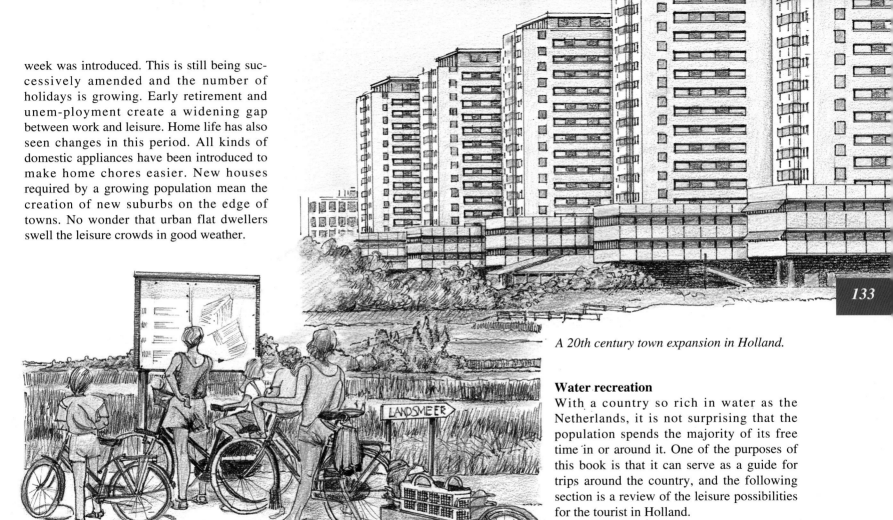

A 20th century town expansion in Holland.

Water recreation

With a country so rich in water as the Netherlands, it is not surprising that the population spends the majority of its free time in or around it. One of the purposes of this book is that it can serve as a guide for trips around the country, and the following section is a review of the leisure possibilities for the tourist in Holland.

133

In the past the rest and "the beehive chair" dominated the North Sea beach. Every day was a Sunday!

The North Sea coast

For the beach lover, the North Sea coast is Eldorado. For tourists looking for a more restful environment, the islands of Texel, Terschelling, Vlieland, Ameland and Schiermonnikoog are out-of-season havens of rest. Visitors to Vlieland have to leave their cars on the mainland. A fast ferryboat serves Vlieland on its way to Terschelling,

The North Sea coast boasts wide sandy beeches and a cooling sea breeze.

Zandvoort by the sea.

the crossing taking forty-five minutes. The islands offer the opportunity for cycling and walking. The Waddenzee lies in the shelter of the island chain and at low tide it is dry attracting migratory birds on their way south. There are walking tours across the wad in charge of an experienced guide.

The Dutch beaches are wide and in spite of the cooling breeze, ideal for the many sunbathers. The ancient beach chairs have been replaced by spacious beach huts and beach bars and restaurants.

The sea provides countless possibilities for active recreation. The conditions for surfing and sailing are excellent and outside the season beach walking is a popular pastime.

The North-Holland coast

At the extreme tip of North-Holland lies the town of Den Helder and the naval base. It is well known for the annual Open Fleet Day. Warships can be visited and demonstrations

Fort Kijkduin at Huisduinen.

The harbour at Harlingen.

Ferryboats from Den Helder, the Friesian- and Groningen coast serve the North Sea islands.

are given for the public. A new feature near Den Helder is Fort Kijkduin at Huisduinen. The historical fort was built by emperor Napoleon two hundred years ago and has been recently restored and provided with restaurants and a unique sea-aquarium. Further south along the coast is the attractive town of Bergen, which hosted a famous artists' colony in the twenties. For a spectacular view of the large ocean-going ships entering and leaving the North Sea Canal travel still further south to IJmuiden. The fish is of excellent quality here and a walk along the new yacht marina can be recommended.

Zandvoort, Noordwijk, Katwijk, Scheveningen and Hoek van Holland are lovely, busy and wellknown sea-side resorts. Especially Scheveningen with its pier and monumental "Kurhaus" still exudes the atmosphere of bygone glory. A visit to the miniature town of Madurodam and the Panorama Mesdag in nearby Den Haag is not to be missed.

South- Holland and Zeeland islands coast
The South- Holland island of Voorne's coast

is an attractive nature reserve. The beaches are extensive and for a stretch of ten kilometres at least a hundred metres wide. The dunes are very varied: drift dunes, dune lakes, shrubbery and woods. This forms the habitat for many different bird sorts and a varied plant life. Built against the sea dune are the towns of Rockanje and Oostvoorne. There are many different kinds of recreation along the coast. On the Zeeland islands are

136

1. Kurhaus at Scheveningen 2. Doris Rijkers at IJmuiden 3. A groyne extending into the North Sea 4. Madurodam in Den Haag 5. Sailing ships, North Sea Canal.

the pleasant resorts of Renesse, Domburg and Westkapelle, and on the point of Zeeuws-Vlaanderen, the town of Cadzand.

The large Delta lakes
As described in chapter 4, after the 1953 flood disaster the Delta project was set up to close the sea arms. This changed the way of life in the Delta for good. The new highways passing over the dams have broken the

The coast of Walcheren in Zeeland.

The yacht harbour "Port Zeelande".

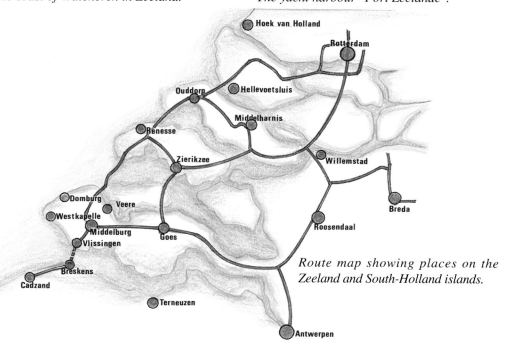

Route map showing places on the Zeeland and South-Holland islands.

The waters of Zeeland are ideal for all kinds of water sport.

View of the old city gate at Zierikzee.

isolation of Zeeland and made it more accessible for visitors. There is a lot of sailing activity on the Delta lakes. Many of the small towns only later cashed in on the tourist industry, and in this way have managed to retain their intrinsic charm. A good example of this is Hellevoetsluis, the old naval harbour on the Haringvliet. Willemstad, near the Moerdijk bridge, is an interesting old fortified town. Veere and Vlissingen (Flushing) with its view from the harbour front across the wide Westerschelde are also worth a visit.

The IJsselmeer

For the water sport fan looking for a more restful location, the IJsselmeer with its associated peripheral lakes, offers a great

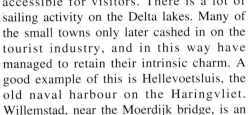

The harbour front at Vlissingen

Watersport at Veere.

View of Volendam.

The outdoor museum at Enkhuizen.

The entry lock to Friesland at Stavoren.

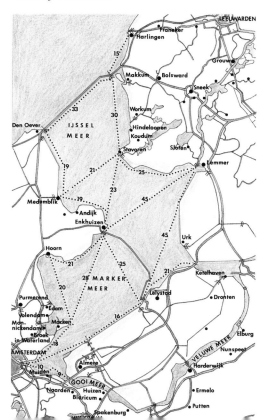

The historic old harbour at Hoorn.

East Indiaman "Batavia" from Lelystad.

many possibilities on the water. There are the resque towns of Hoorn, Enkhuizen, Medemblik, Edam and Volendam. The Outdoor museum at Enkhuizen is a "must". It portrays the culture and way of life of the Zuiderzee region as it once was. Trips across the enclosing dike to the Friesian coast, or across the connecting dike from Enkhuizen to Lelystad, are bound to impress. Here a replica of the seventeenth century East Indiaman "the Batavia" has been built, and it lies in the Zuiderzee Museum which displays a collection of all the finds from the former Zuiderzee.

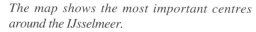
The map shows the most important centres around the IJsselmeer.

The rivers of the Delta

The rivers and their flood plains form a unique landscape with its own characteristic beauty. This Lowland has much to offer. The variety existing within such a tiny area is startling. Nijmegen, situated on the Waal, has preserved the ruins of the "Valkhof" dating from the time of Charles

Nijmegen on the Waal has a special atmosphere.

A farm behind the dike of the river Lek.

Fortified town of Heusden on the Meuse.

the Great.

Driving across the bridge at Nijmegen one has a glorious view of the Betuwe, which is a burst of blossom in the spring. As a result of quarrying and river truncation, all kinds of water-based recreation take place along the course of the river. In the Bommelerwaard is the old Loevestein Castle, famous for the imprisonment there of Hugo de Groot, and for his escape in an empty bookchest.

For a fine example of a small fortified town, one need look no further than Heusden on the lovely Bergsche Meuse. The interesting nature recreation area of the Biesbosch is close by.

The river de Linge is an ideal location for active recreation.

Canoeing on the Linge

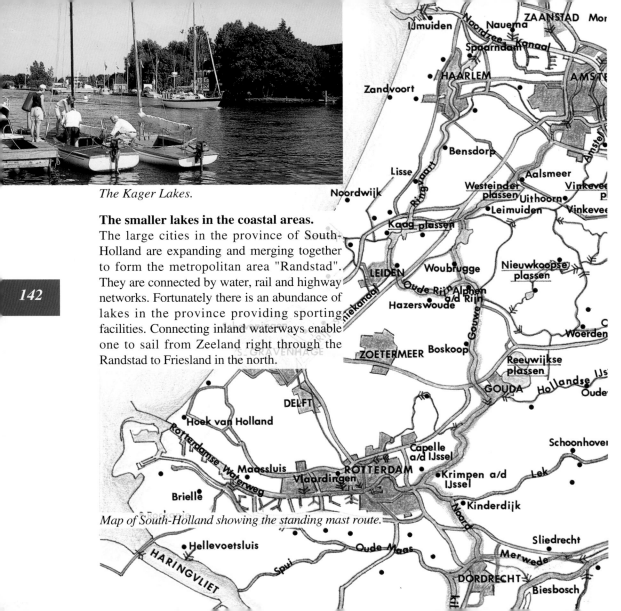

The Kager Lakes.

The smaller lakes in the coastal areas.

The large cities in the province of South-Holland are expanding and merging together to form the metropolitan area "Randstad". They are connected by water, rail and highway networks. Fortunately there is an abundance of lakes in the province providing sporting facilities. Connecting inland waterways enable one to sail from Zeeland right through the Randstad to Friesland in the north.

Map of South-Holland showing the standing mast route.

Waterways were important in the past for a town. (On the picture Leiden).

As a result of peat digging in the past, many lakes have appeared in the low-lying parts of Holland. They have been discovered by water sport enthusiasts. The Westeinder and Kager Lakes are well known, but the Vinkeveen and Loosdrecht Lakes are also popular. The river Vecht near Utrecht is well known for the mansions and gardens built along its banks. This was a popular location for rich Amsterdam merchants to build their

Handsome mansions built along the Vecht.

Sailing on the Friesian Lakes.

summerhouses allowing their families to escape from the suffocating city.

The lakes in Friesland are among the best in the country, and Friesland is a strong water sport province.

An annual sailing event is "Skuutsje sielen" involving races by the large flat-bottomed sailing barges. In the winter the province is famous for its skating events culminating in the "Elfstedentocht".

Skaters in a winter landscape.

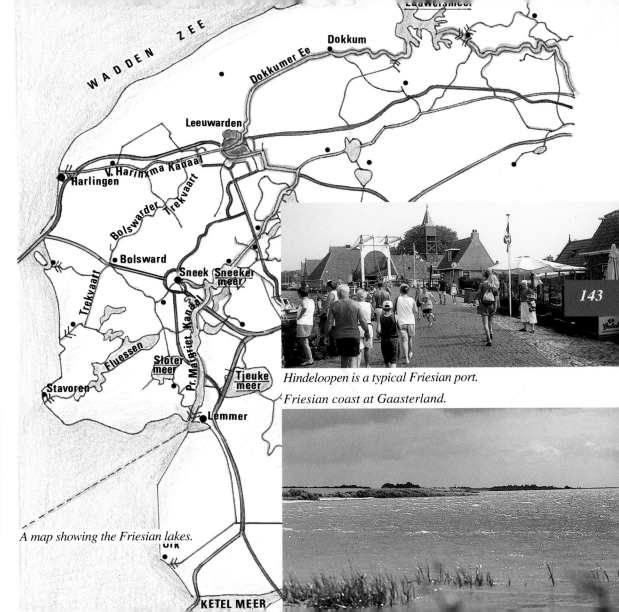
A map showing the Friesian lakes.

Hindeloopen is a typical Friesian port.

Friesian coast at Gaasterland.

11 | MUSEA

The Netherlands is a country of museums. Although a strict selection has been applied, the chosen locations add an extra dimension to the subject matter of this book.

The Zuiderzeemuseum in Enkhuizen

Besides the museum building there is an open-air museum. The old museum is housed in a row of historical buildings at Westdijk number 18. One of the buildings, a 17th century pepper warehouse, belonged to the former Associated East India Company. The trading port of Enkhuizen was very important for Amsterdam.

The historical whaling industry is one of the topics featured in the museum. The

The open air museum in Enkhuizen.

open- air museum gives a very nice and educational impression of the past Zuiderzee culture.

"Maeslantkering" at Hoek van Holland

The imposing river barrage "Maeslantkering" is the last link in the Delta Scheme. From the control room there is a view across the New Waterway and over the whole of the barrage complex. If a sea flood threatens then the two massive doors are closed to protect the hinterland of South Holland. If travelling by car take the N 220 on the Maasdijk in the direction of Hoek of Holland. Leave the road at the sign for "Industrieterrein de Hoek" and follow signs to "Maeslantkering" or dock number 881.

Miniature City of Madurodam

Madurodam is an exact scale replica (1:25)

Maeslantkering in the Nieuwe Waterweg.

of buildings and structures to be found in the major Dutch cities. By walking through the park the visitor is presented with a bird's eye view of the architecture and infrastructure of the Netherlands. Young and old will be captured by this miniature city.

The Poldermuseum in Lelystad gives a good idea of the winning of new land.

New Land Poldermuseum, Lelystad

The museum is housed in a building of remarkable design situated on newly reclaimed land that just a generation ago was the bed of the Zuiderzee. The permanent exhibits tell the story of a century-long struggle of the inhabitants of the Lowlands with the sea. It is a hectic story of dike building, dike breaching and making the land free from danger. These events are reproduced for the visitor using original film and sound recordings. Besides models there are interactive computer programmes and an exciting multi-media show "Waterland". Historical films can be viewed by special request. A visit to the museum is an adventure and at the same time a lesson in how a small country can excel.

The Dutch Water Museum

The Dutch Water Museum (2003) is going to be housed at a splendid location, the "Be-gijnemolen" (Beguine Mill) in Arnhem's monumental city park Sonsbeek. In and under this historically valuable water mill the visitor will find a new- largely underground- building with a total surface area of 2500 m2. The Dutch Water Museum will be a splashy action museum offering information on all aspects of fresh water in a sparkling way. In addition to its permanent exhibition there is a collection of cultural heritage to be discovered, and the knowledge and documentation centre of the new museum is the very place to come to with any questions in the field of fresh water. Besides the serious material the museum offers lots of water fun as well. In front of the grand-Café a water play- area will be arranged where children can enjoy themselves while gaining their own experience with water control.

Open Air Museum Arnhem

The way of life of simple vocations such as farming, crafts and manual labour, are brought to life in the open-air museum in Arnhem.

Het Nederlands Watermuseum te Sonsbeek.

The open air museum in Arnhem.

There are very few artefacts surviving from these social groups simply because they tended to use their belongings until they were worn out. Because little attention was paid to this "social history", many of the buildings such as farms, barns, houses and mills have disappeared. Fortunately, as a result of initiatives of the open-air museum, characteristic buildings from the various regions of the Netherlands have been saved and moved to the Museum Park. The interiors have been carefully restored and it is possible to step inside into another world.

Water, the theme of this publication, manifests itself in quite a different way. The process of papermaking using water is demonstrated live in a mill on the site. An old laundry from Overveen displays the industrial process of washing.

Overveen lies at the foot of the dunes in

Kennemerland. This area was well known for its pure dune water and the washed textile could be laid out to dry on the grassy areas behind the dunes. There was a good market for the laundry because well-to-do families had long been established in these pleasant surroundings.

In the farm buildings from Friesland the farmers wife is making butter and cheese, whilst the steam powered dairy "Freia" demonstrates how the world famous Dutch dairy produce was made. One of the oldest herb gardens has been reproduced in the museum growing kitchen and medicinal herbs. Especially in late summer the air here is filled with rich fragrance. During the season there are innumerable craft demonstrations to interest both young and old alike. The museum is situated on the northern side of Arnhem near the A12/E35.

Panorama Mesdag

A visitor to the Netherlands always has to take account of changeable weather conditions, and for this reason Panorama Mesdag at Zeestraat 65b in The Hague with its indoor viewing platform is an appropriate address in any weather. The formation of the dune coastline has been

Panorama Mesdag in The Hague.

described in the Compass. These days in the summer months we are used to the phenomenon of the beach being occupied by seaside visitors. Yet the 19th century panorama at Mesdag shows us a completely different picture. The panoramic cylindrical shaped screen shows the fishing village of Scheveningen and its beach in the year 1880 viewed from a dune top. The painting is 120 metres in length and 4 metres in height and its diameter is 36 metres. The fishing smacks are drawn up on the beach ready to put to sea.

On another part of the beach, the cavalry are exercising on horseback. As we turn our gaze inland the old village of Scheveningen comes into view. The viewing platform is accessible via a stair within the cylinder. The surprise of the panoramic view together with the sounds of

the waves breaking on the beach and the cries of the gulls is so complete that it is difficult to realise that it is just a painting. Panorama Mesdag is one of the few preserved panoramas which were very popular with the European public in the 19th century. It was a popular Sunday afternoon diversion to take the children to see a panorama. We must remember that there were few other attractions in that time. There were no illustrated magazines and colour photography had not yet been developed, and ordinary people were not able to travel as they do now. Talented painters such as H.W. Mesdag and his wife S. Mesdag-van Houten, Th. De Block and G.M. Breitner all worked on this colossal undertaking. The rotunda, which was built specially for the panorama in 1880, was opened to the public in 1881. Included in the museum complex are a number of galleries exhibiting paintings, watercolours and studies by H.W. Mesdag and S. Mesdag-van Houten.

Maritime Museums

Since 1973 the Maritime Museum has been established in the Admiralty storehouse on the Kattenburgerplein in Amsterdam. In

The Maritime Museum in Amsterdam.

front of the building is moored a replica of the 18th century three-masted ship the "Amsterdam". The museum collection gives a good impression of the naval history of the Netherlands; the state of the nation, the various wars and sea battles, and the types of naval vessel. The Dutch naval heritage of industry and culture is on display: from coastal fishing to foreign trade, from shipbuilding to seamanship. The Museum has an extensive collection of ship models, paintings, flags, figureheads, nautical instruments, atlases and globes. There is a library of 50,000 books including many 17th and 18th century volumes, notes and archivalia.

Since 1986, the Prins Hendrik Museum in

Rotterdam has been housed in a strikingly modern building designed by the architect W. Quist. The building is situated on the quayside of the Leuvehaven where H.M. "Buffel", a restored 19th century naval vessel, is moored. Until 1896 this ship was in service guarding the Dutch coast. The interior reflects the style of the second half of the 19th century. The officers' quarters, the decorated upper deck and decorations on the hull are particularly impressive.

Windmills at Kinderdijk
Kinderdijk is near Rotterdam at the North-western point of Alblasserwaard. As many as 19 smock mills were built here around 1740 to drain the polder. All of them are still there in their original surroundings and that is the reason they are included on the UNESCO world heritage list.

Impressive mill collection at Kinderdijk.

The fishing museum of Vlaardingen.

These tower mills are typical of the South-Holland polder pumping mills. The characteristic tail is a wooden beam for turning the cap and its sails into the wind. The North-Holland version of this mill has a more sober appearance because the turning mechanism is inside. When the mills are in operation they demonstrate the dynamics of shifting quantities of water by a flight of mills from the low-lying polders into the river Lek.

The Fishery Museum at Vlaardingen
The Netherlands Sea fishing Institute is located on the Westhaven at Vlaardingen, close to Rotterdam. It is accommodated in a patrician's house, "the house with the Linden tree" dating from 1740. There is a seawater basin and an aquarium in the museum. With the help of scale models and

photographs the development of the Dutch fishing industry is traced. Dioramas explain the techniques of fishing and the equipment employed. The social conditions and traditional costumes of the fishing community are on display. There is a library and a photo' and print archive as well as a collection of technical drawings.

Neeltje Jans (Zeeland)
The Delta Expo is located on the former work island Neeltje Jans near Burgh-Haamstede in Zeeland. The presentation in the expo covers not only the Delta Scheme but also a history of Dutch water management. There is an instructive boat trip around the estuary of the Ooster-schelde and a guided tour of the Oos-terschelde barrage. The recently constructed pavilion, which resembles a stranded whale, houses an audio-video

The Neeltje Jans Expo.

The steam engine "The Cruquius".

presentation of the water cycle in all its aspects.

Steam pumping station "De Cruquius"
For those with an interest in water management and especially in the steam age, this museum is a special attraction. The Cruquius, situated on the ring canal in Heemstede, is one of the three oldest classic pumping stations that together drained the Haarlem Lake. The international airport Schiphol owes its location in one corner of the former lake to the success of this operation. As described in the main text this station was in operation from 1849 till 1933. The steam engine in the Cruquius is one of the largest of its kind, a so-called "Cornish Engine". It is now fitted out as an educational museum for hydraulics, polders and drainage

systems. There are models, drawings and maps on exhibit and continuous films about water management. Should you have a wider interest in steam matters then the **Netherlands Steam Engine Museum "De Vier Noorder Koggen"** at Medemblik is a must. The industrial revolution (1750-1820) saw the application of steam power for all possible purposes. The steam pumping station at Medemblik was controlling water levels in the north of the country until 1976.
The Wouda pumping station at Lemmer.

Wouda pumping engine at Lemmer (Fr).
Finally a look at the largest steam pumping engine in Europe appearing on the Unesco world heritage list. The engine was opened on 7th October 1920 by Queen Wilhelmina and is still operational. It is equipped with four 650 h.p compound steam engines

The Wouda pumping station at Lemmer.

working in tandem and each driving two centrifugal pumps. In 1955 the original boilers were replaced by four Stork-Werkspoor boilers, and these were converted in 1967 for oil firing. The pumping capacity of the station in normal circumstances is 3900 m3 a minute. In an emergency the capacity can be increased to 4150 m3 a minute. The pumping station owes its name to the engineer Dirk Frederik Wouda. The Unesco describes the still operational station as "an outstanding example of the contribution of Dutch engineers and architects to the defence of a country and its inhabitants against flooding." The station is operated by the water authority "Wetterskip Fryslân".

The Archeon (Zuid Holland)
The theme park "Archeon" is located on the edge of Alphen a/d Rijn. The aim of the park is to give visitors an active impression of archaeology. This science is concerned with the finds emerging from under the ground surface. Experts analyse these artefacts and their location with a view to clarifying historical development.

Often new material is revealed during building construction works. New legislation requires access to be given to such sites by archaeo-logists. At Archeon, the experts are given the opportunity to at least reconstruct a fraction of their discoveries in the form of buildings.

Not only are prehistoric times represented here, there is also a Roman bath and temple and a village from the Middle Ages. In the summer season, a child can learn more here in one visit than in a year at school.

The Archeon at Alphen a/d Rijn.

National Museum of Dredging at Sliedrecht.

National Museum of Dredging (Z-H).
The museum is housed in a stately home on the Molendijk in Sliedrecht. Both the past and present state of the industry is represented here. Dutch dredging prowess is world-renowned and their contribution to harbour works is evident in most maritime countries. The museum collection is very impressive; from ship models to objects retrieved during dredging; from original dredging brace to the steam-dredging engine. The museum brings the whole story of dredging to life.

Castles
A description of four water castles is included; Muiderslot; Loevestein; Radboud and the ruins of Brederode, all worth a visit. *The Muiderslot* gives an almost complete picture of a water castle in residence.

Het Muiderslot (N.H.).

The castle was built on a strategic location at the mouth of the River Vecht by Count Floris V. It is fitted out with 17th century furnishings from the time that the poet P.C. Hooft was lord of the castle. He made the castle a centre of the arts and sciences. A group of leading figures met here regularly and has since come to be known in Dutch history as the "Muiderkring". The **Slot Loevestein** was built around 1360 at the confluence of the rivers Meuse and Waal. During the 17th century the castle was in use as a state prison. It became famous for the incarceration of the lawyer Hugo de Groot, whose spectacular escape after two years' imprisonment has become part of Dutch history. **Castle Radboud** also dates from the time of Count Floris V who used the castle as a fortress in his repression of the West Friesians.

In the course of time the castle deteriorated until part of it was restored at the end of the 19th century. The keep of **Castle Brederode** has been well preserved but the rest is a romantic ruin. Following the fall of the city of Haarlem in 1573 during the 80 years war, the Duke of Alva commanded his Spanish troops to blow up the castle. Since that time the structure has remained a romantic ruin.

Fortified towns

Under this heading there are a number of attractive Dutch towns where the science of defence works can be studied. The stone walls of castle and town were no longer a match for the improving artillery.

Menno v Coehoorn (1641-1704) succeeded in designing fortifications in the form of

Fortified town of Bourtange, SE Groningen.

Fortified town of Willemstad.

earthworks. A fine example of his work is to be found at the town of **Bourtange** in Southeast Groningen. At the time it was one of the most important fortifications in the northern part of the country, and it has been totally restored. The fortified town of **Naarden** guarded the southeastern approach to Amsterdam and has been preserved in good condition. A museum has been established in the fort. In the underground dungeons life-size models showing military situations are on exhibit and in the museum all kinds of uniforms, weaponry, photographs, engravings and prints are on display. The fort was in service during the period 1685 to 1926. The star-shaped defences can be seen most clearly from the air.

Willemstad

This is also a well-preserved fortified town strategically situated at the confluence of the Haringvliet and the Hollands Diep, close to the modern day Hellegatsplein. Thanks to the intact defence works, Willemstad is a landscaped city and has fine walks along the landscaped walls. The evolution of defence works in the period 1583-1945 is clearly evident at Willemstad. It is not surprising that in 1970 the town was declared a conservation area.

Hellevoetsluis

The last of our list of fortified towns is also situated on the Haringvliet, but more to the west than Willemstad, not far from the Haringvliet dam. Besides being a fortified town, Hellevoetsluis was also a naval harbour, a unique combination.

The fort of Vijfhuizen.

The Amsterdam defence line

Finally a description of the culmination of a centuries long development to create a defence line around Amsterdam. The cordon of forts and waterworks has achieved international recognition since its placement in 1996 on the Unesco world heritage list.

The listing of this monumental work implies a responsibility for the upkeep of all the forts and waterworks which are now more than 100 years old. In 2002 **Fort Vijfhuizen** will be completely restored as part of the Floriade to be held here. It will be a jewel in the Amsterdam defence line, and will be equipped as visitor centre and central information point for all 42 of the forts in the cordon around the capital Amsterdam.

Visitor Centres in the dunes (N-H)

The dunes area is important not only as a sea defence but also for water supply and recreation. There are several visitor centres in the North-Holland dunes area, which are worth a visit. The best known is "**de Hoep**" at Castricum, operated by the PWN Water Supply Company. The reservation is 5300 hectares in extent. A more recently opened centre is *"de Zandwaaier"* in the Kennemerduinen National Park. In this centre, the relationship between flora, fauna and their natural environment is highlighted. Updated exhibitions, audio-visual presentations, films and modern media, as well as excursions with an expert guide are there to inform and excite the visitors' interest. A large area of dunes to the south of the centre managed by the *Amsterdam water supply Company* is a paradise for walkers. There is also a smaller visitor centre at the pumping station Oranjekom, Vogelenzang entrance.

Visitor centre "de Hoep" at Castricum.

BIBLIOGRAPHY

There is a multitude of publications on this subject. Listed below in alphabetical order are the main titles used as reference for this work.

Bakker, P.;
 Wij en het water, *Meppel.*
Boonenburg,K.;
 De Zuiderzee, *Amsterdam, 1956.*
Brand, H.; Brand, J.;
 De Hollandse Waterlinie, *Utrecht/Antwerpen, 1986.*
Constandse, A.K.;
 Planning en Vormgeving, *Lelystad, 1976.*
Elffers, J.; Schuyt, M.; Overbeek, A.;
 Groot Museumboek, *Amsterdam 1980.*
Uni van Waterschappen;
 Den Haag, 1998.
Groen, K.; Schmeink, T.;
 Dijken, *Den Haag, 1985.*
Heslinga, M.W.; de Klerk, A.P.; Schmal, H.;
Stol, T.; Thurkow, A.J.;
 Nederland in kaarten, *Ede, 1985.*
Kosman, H.;
 Drinken uit de plas, *Amsterdam, 1988.*
Lambooij, H.;
 Getekend Land, *Alkmaar 1978.*
Loomeijer, F.R.;
 De Nederlandse visserij 1900-1935, *Alkmaar, 1995.*
Schaap, D.;
 Halen en brengen, *Alphen a/d Rijn, 1978.*
Schilstra, J.J.;
 Wie water deert, *Bergen, 1969.*
Ven, van de, G.P.;
 Leefbaar Laagland, *Den Haag, 1993.*

ACKNOWLEDGEMENTS

PHOTO'S AND ILLUSTRATIONS

Fot.(blz.39,44,72 en 121),
 Spaarnestad Fotoarchief, *Haarlem.*
Fot. (blz.16,33,34),
 Atlas van Stolk, *Rotterdam.*
*2 Fot.(blz.88); 1 fot.(blz.90); 2 Fot.(blz.91); 1
Fot.(blz.103),*
 Visserij Museum, *Vlaardingen.*
*1 Fot.(blz.35); 3 Fot.(blz.36); 2 Fot.(blz.37); 1
Fot.(blz.71); 1 Fot.(blz.79); 1 Fot.(blz.110); 1
Fot.(blz.111); 1 Fot.(blz.114),*
 Rijksarchief, *Noord-Holland.*
Fot. (blz.67),
 Amsterdam Water Supply.
Fot. (blz.89),
 Panorama Mesdag, *Den Haag.*
2 Fot. (blz. 63, 144), Rijkswaterstaat, *Den Haag.*
Fot. (blz. 145), Nederlands watermuseum, *Arnhem.*
Fot. (blz. 145), Nieuwland poldermuseum, *Lelystad.*
Ill.(blz.8/9),
 naar Archeologische cahiers, ROB, 1985.
Ill. (blz.10),
 naar Nieuwe kaart Hollands Noorderkwartier in 1350,
Alkmaar.
Ill. (blz.12),
 naar een heruitgegeven kaart v. Zeeland omstreeks 1300,
Zierikzee, 1983.
Ill. (blz.14/15),
 naar een oude schoolplaat, Groningen.
Ill. (blz.16),
 eveneens een schoolplaat, Groningen.

Ill. (blz.52,53,55,58),
 publicaties Rijkswaterstaat, Den Haag.
Ill. (blz.95,97,98,99), Rivo IJmuiden.
*) PHOTO'S AND ILLUSTRATIONS
The sketched illustrations were for a large part based on illustrations from an educational clipping dossier. It is impossible to trace the source of the illustrations. Persons wishing to claim rights should contact the publisher. The clipping dossier has been supplemented and the subject matter of Holland Compass has been updated by the use of current press releases.

COLOFON

Subject matter advice:
*W.Timp; P.IJff; A.J.Roebert; F.Veenstra en F.H. de Wit;
J. Stuip; C. Evertsen*
Marketing and communication:
J.C.M. Hoep-van Buuren
Layout and production:
V.H. Hoep
Design, text, illustrations and slides:
F.S.Hoep
Design cover:
O. IJ. Cosijn
English translation:
A.L. Barker
Printing and DTP service and finalisation:
Drukkerij Nivo, Delft

With gratitude to:

By their subscription to a quaranteed number of copies, the following firms and organisations have made this translation into English possible and are helping to promote Holland and its socio- historical background in English- speaking countries. These firms are all involved in the business of water.

 Vereniging van Waterbouwers en Bagger- Kust en Oeverwerken

 P&O Nedlloyd

 Alterra

 Nuon

 Ministerie van Verkeer en Waterstaat

 Haskoning

 van Oord

 Nederlands Instituut voor Visserij Onderzoek

The publisher of Holland Compass would like to express thanks for their contribution.

Adres   : Marnixstraat 46, 2023 RE Haarlem
Telephone : +31 23 525 15 87
Telefax   : +31 23 525 45 75
Web site   : www.hollandkompas.com

ISBN 90-801454-2-4